Form and Content in Commercial Music

Christopher P. Gordon
Mississippi University for Women

Ardsley House, Publishers, Inc.
New York

Address orders and editorial
correspondence to:
Ardsley House, Publishers, Inc.
320 Central Park West
New York, NY 10025

ISBN: 1-880157-01-2

Printed in the United States of America

10 9 8 7 6 5 4 3 2 1

This book is dedicated to the memory of
Dr. Fred Prentice,
Professor Emeritus at the University of Alabama,
who shaped a generation of pupils,
and to my wife, Pam,
and my children, Anna and Victoria,
who inspire me and make my life abundant.

Contents

Preface   xi

Introduction   1

Part One   *Basics*   3

   1   **Intervals**   5

      Major Scales   5
      Intervals in the Major Scale   7
      Compound Intervals   7
      Projects   8

   2   **Scales**   9

      Communication with the Listener   9
      Modes   10
      Scales Used as Tonal Centers   12
         Major Scales 12
         Key Signatures 14
         Minor Scales 17
         Other Scales 24
      Projects   25

3   Chord Spelling   **26**

   Numbering Notes   26
   Constructing Triads   27
   Types of Triads   30
   Diatonic Chords   31
   Projects   32

4   Seventh Chords   **33**

   Seventh Intervals   34
   Projects   35

Part Two   *Harmony*   **37**

5   Chord Functions   **39**

   Intervals and Harmonic Motion   39
   Tonic   40
   Dominant   41
   Subdominant   42
   Projects   43

6   Chord Extensions   **44**

   Chord-Symbol Notation   44
   Use of Ninths   45
   Use of Elevenths   46
   Alterations of Fifths   48
   Use of Thirteenths   48
   The $\frac{9}{6}$ Chord   49
   Projects   50

7   Chord Voicing   **52**

   Closed/Open Position   52
   Drop 2   53
   Drop 2 and 4   54
   Quartal/4th Voicings   54
   Clusters   55
   Other Open-Position Voicings   56
   Projects   57

8   Voice Leading   **58**

   Movement from Chord to Chord   58
   Guide Tones   59

Movement within the Same Chord   61
Projects   62

9   Modulations   **64**

Why Isn't Everything in C Major?   64
Which Key Should I Go To?   65
How Do I Change Keys?   67
   Surprise Modulation 67
   V and Go 68
   Prepared Modulation 69
Projects   72

10   Chord Substitution   **73**

Subdominant Chords   73
Dominant Chords   74
Neapolitan Substitution (Tritone Substitution)   75
ii⁷-V⁷-I   75
Projects   78

11   Further Substition   **80**

V⁷sus   80
ii of the Neapolitan   81
Polychords   83
Planing   84
Nonfunctional, Passing Harmony Techniques   85
   Linear Relationships 85
   Vertical Relationships 86
Diatonic Inversion of Chords   88
Projects   88

12   Pedal Points and Ostinato   **90**

Pedal Pont   90
Ostinato   93
Projects   95

Part Three   *Melody*   **97**

13   Melodic Manipulation   **99**

Melodic Construction   99
Basic Elements   100

Repetition   100
Augmentation and Diminution   103
Inversion and Retrograde   104
Transportation and Fragmentation   105
Sequences   106
Nonharmonic Tones   107
    Weak-Beat Nonharmonic Tones 107
    Strong-Beat Nonharmonic Tones 110
Rhythmic Displacement   112
Changing Time Signatures   114
Projects   115

14   Melodic Contour   **118**

Melodic Rhythm   118
Composing a Motive or Hook   120
Melodic Shape   121
Tension and Release (Leaps and Skips)   121
Phase Structure   122
Composing a Melody   123
Projects   124

15   Melodies from Scales and Modes   **126**

Modes   126
    The Ionian Mode 126
    The Dorian Mode 127
    The Phrygian Mode 127
    The Lydian Mode 128
    The Mixolydian Mode 128
    The Aeolian Mode 128
    The Locrian Mode 129
Harmony and Its Corresponding Modes   129
Other Scales   130
Modal Alterations   133
Projects   134

Part Four   *Form*   **135**

16   Blues   **137**

Rural Blues   137
Urban Blues   138
Harmony   138

Melody   139
Projects   140

17   The Popular Song   **141**

Songs That Last   141
Labeling System   142
A-A-A Form   143
A-A^1-B-A Form   143
Hybrids of the 32-Bar Song Form   144
    A-B-A-B 144
    A-B-A-C 145
    A-B-C-D 145
    A-A-B 145
Song Forms in Contemporary Production   145
Projects   146

18   Jingles and Advertising   **147**

Jingles   148
The Image Statement   150
Film Scoring   151
    Concepts in Film Scoring 151
Projects   153

19   TV and Film   **154**

The Role of Music   154
Scoring Drama   155
Main Titles/Closing Credits   156
Feature Songs   157
Projects   158

Part Five   *Orchestration*   **159**

20   Acoustic Orchestration   **161**

The Percussion Family   162
    Drums 162
    Wooden Percussion Instruments 163
    Metallic Percussion Instruments 163
    Melodic Percussion Instruments 163
    Cymbals 163
    Other Percusion Instruments 164
    Functions of Percussion Instruments 164

The String Family   165
The Brass Family   165
The Woodwind Family   167
    The Flute Family 167
    The Single Reeds 167
    The Double Reeds 169
The Keyboard Instruments   170
    The Harp 171
Fretted Instruments   171
The Voice Family   172
Projects   173

21   Electronic Orchestration   **174**

Technology and the Musician   174
Synthesizers   175
    Analog Synthesizers 175
    Digital Synthesizers 175
Sampling   175
Sequencing   176
Effects   176
Concepts in Electronic Orchestration   176
Projects   177

Appendix   *Interviews*   **179**

Interview with Gino Vannelli   181
Interview with Dan Fogelberg   199
Interview with Doug Wilde   211
Interview with Mike Post   231

Bibliography   251

Index   253

Preface

This book has been written to fill two needs in my classroom. The academic need was to give young music students a scholarly understanding of the mechanics and language of music. The professional need was for academic music training to promote later professional productivity of lasting quality and worth. My goal was to bring the two worlds closer together. I hope neither has been compromised.

An Introduction to Form and Content in Commercial Music is a theory text that presents basic structural concepts, from the rudimental to the more advanced, in such a way that students can see these concepts functioning within music more familiar to them than that of two hundred years ago. In this manner, students can focus on understanding these structural concepts without the added burden of simultaneously interpreting foreign literature. This is not to say that the masters of the past should be cast aside for the most modern of popular-music composers. It is merely a new approach to the introduction of already complex material to young people in a way that is more accessible to them. When a minimum degree of structural understanding has been acquired, the intense study of the former masters' works will be essential for continued musical growth.

The book may also be used as a guide for training budding composers and arrangers. I feel that this volume presents an opportunity to scan the musical possibilities that await the next generation of professional writers and players. Even though the scope of the book is an overview of the musical content of the American popular culture and does not pretend to be a definitive treatise in this area, it may serve as an introduction to the field of professional music in a manner not previously attempted.

My goal and sincere wish is that a student accept none of the techniques suggested within these covers as the only possible devices for solving musical problems. Only through the student's own playing and writing experience can any concept be proven or disproven to be useful and valid. These chapters have been written from my experience and from that of many others; yet, only through the individual student's productivity can there be true lessons learned. In the words of a former teacher, Ross Lee Finney, "Write, and write a lot!"

Acknowledgements

This book was written with the gracious help of Dr. Prince L. Dorough, Dan Fogelberg, Dr. Horace G. Gordon, Dave Hanson, Instructor of Music at Denver University, Dr. Richard Montalto, Assistant Professor of Music at Mississippi University for Women, Jerry Oleaf, Mike Post, Steve Sample, Professor of Music at The University of Alabama, Gino Vannelli, Dena Wallenstein, and Doug Wilde, as well as the Faculty Development Committee at Mississippi University for Women. It was also made possible through the knowledge gained from musicians I've worked with, teachers I've learned from, friends I've grown to love, and students I've taught. And finally, to my parents and extended family, for their constant support, a most heartfelt thank you.

CHRISTOPHER P. GORDON

Form and Content in Commercial Music

Introduction

Commercial music is a huge field that offers many exciting opportunities for the aspiring musician. Music is an essential part of the advertising industry, helping to promote an image or attach a memorable slogan to a product. Television shows often have new scores written for each episode, and film scoring can be crucial for dramatic and structural effects. Furthermore, there is a large and varied market for musicians who simply want to write and/or perform popular music: jazz, blues, rock, and so on.

Form and Content in Commercial Music will speak to you about just that—the marriage of form and content with the commercial-music industries. The importance of a formal background in music theory cannot be underestimated. This is stressed again and again by successful commercial musicians, such as those interviewed in this book:

Gino Vannelli: You can't just listen to music—you have to have some formal background, an understanding of the basics of the laws, and if you want to break them or use them, whatever.

Doug Wilde: Listen in as many different ways as you can . . . listen to what the rhythm is doing . . . the background harmonies . . . listen in terms of counterpoint . . . texture . . . orchestration . . . In addition to that,

1

write as many different kinds of music as you can and write it as many different ways as you can.

The first half of this book will teach you to understand the structures of music, to recognize the interplay of elements within the music we listen to, and to write your own music, understanding these elements and combining that knowledge with your own creativity and intuition.

The remainder of this book relates this academic knowledge of music to its practical applications. A discussion of the commercial forms mentioned earlier analyzes aspects of this structure and purpose. This is followed by an analysis of the technology of music—from acoustic to electronic orchestration—and of the differences in range, pitch, and tonal quality of different instruments. Finally, interviews with four successful commercial musicians tell us what they do and how (and why) they do it.

Part One
Basics

1

Intervals

Our discussion of the structure of music starts with the basic unit called the **interval**—the difference in pitch between two tones, created when any two notes are played simultaneously or consecutively. The interval is identified by a number, indicating the relative distance between the two notes, and an adjective name, indicating the quality or specific distance of the interval.

Major Scales

Scales or **modes** are units of pitch arranged in specific orders of half steps and whole steps. The various modes and scales will be outlined in the next chapter. We now concentrate on the major scale for our discussion of intervals. In a **major scale** there are seven pitches making up the scale. If each scale member were to be numbered, 1–7, a numerical name may be attached to each interval, or distance, created in the space between the first scale member, or 1, and any other scale member, 2–7. In other words, the distance between the first degree of the scale and the fifth degree of the scale would be called a fifth.

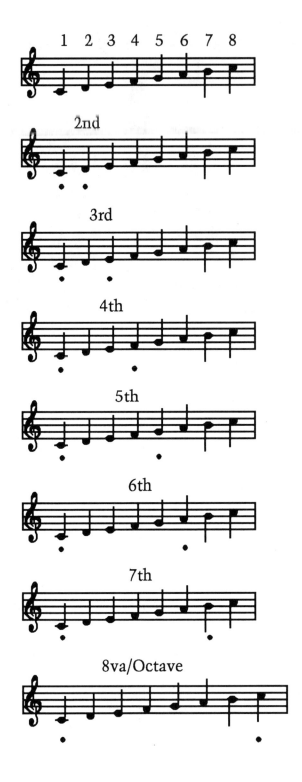

The numerical name for any interval serves as a generic or family name due to the alphabetic order associated with musical pitches. The distance from G to C is an interval of a fourth because of the alphabetic order, G, A, B, C. There are other pitches that have C as their family name, such as C♯, C♭, C×, and C♭♭. The distances from G to any of these notes are fourths as well. The need for a specific name in conjunction with a generic name for intervals is obvious.

Intervals in the Major Scale

The intervals found in the major scale are as follows: fourths and fifths are **Perfect**; seconds, thirds, sixths, and sevenths are **major**. These are specific names associated with the numerical names in the major scale, and the proper identification of any interval will include both types of adjective. Example: major second, Perfect fifth, etc. The table of interval alteration will indicate which specific interval name is associated with any numerical interval.

Table for Seconds, Thirds, Sixths, and Sevenths	Table for Fourths and Fifths
AUGMENTED	AUGMENTED
MAJOR *	*PERFECT* *
MINOR	DIMINISHED
DIMINISHED	

These terms indicate distance up or down the table in half-step increments. An asterisk indicates how these intervals naturally occur within the major scale.

If the interval C to F is naturally found within the C major scale, it will be called a **Perfect fourth**. If the F were raised to F♯, the interval would be called an **augmented fourth**. If the F were lowered to F♭, the interval would be called a **diminished fourth interval.**

Compound Intervals

When distances between two notes exceed an octave, the interval is regarded as a **compound interval**. To indicate compound intervals, merely add 7 to any scale member. A second + 7 = ninth. The quality of the interval will remain the same—Perfect, major, minor, etc.

1   2   3   4   5   6   7   8   9   10   11   12   13   14   15

PROJECTS

1. Identify a major third up from B♭, D, F♯, G, A, E♭, B, C♯, D♭, and A♭.

2. Identify an augmented fifth up from A; a minor 6th, a Perfect 4th, a major 7th, a diminished 3rd, a minor 9th, an augmented 9th, an augmented 11th, a minor 13th, and a major 9th.

2
Scales

Communication with the Listener

All tonal music is based on the system of chord function and movement within a scale or modality. The arrangements of scales and modes create certain unique aural qualities that are distinctly different from one another. They each have their own psychological effect and degree of exoticism. The factors in the choosing of one scale or mode over another in which to write a melody or derive a harmonic language is centered in the choice of psychological response that is desired from the listener. Herein lies one of the most fundamental of all musical qualities and mysteries, the window and opportunity to affect another through the use of an invisible medium.

This affecting of another individual or group, in their thinking, in their feeling, in their perception of life for a moment, is one of the primary privileges and powers associated with music. This precise point has been the center of debate over its use in society for historic individuals such as Plato and Aristotle and others. In a given moment, when an individual or group voluntarily chooses to open themselves and listen, there exists the opportunity to communicate subjective concepts. These concepts run the gamut of emotions from passion to loyalty, religious fervor to patriotism, bitter loneliness to overpowering love, the warmth of personal nostalgia to the restlessness of uncertainty over the future. These feelings are first expressed in direct proportion to the skill and sensitivity of the composer, and secondly to the performer's desire and ability.

Whether the composition is painstakingly created and planned in isolation awaiting a performer's interpretation at some later time or whether the composition is spontaneous and improvised before a live audience, the composer creates the emotional and psychological communication link to the willing listener; herein lies the power of music. The first step in the creation of this communication bridge lies in the choice of scales or modes. There are several possibilities.

Modes

Modes, or church modes as they are historically called, have a long history of being associated with different psychological powers. The medieval church went so far as to establish rules of modal usage in liturgical music, the very center of sociological and musical activity at the time. For our purposes, the modes are: the **Ionian** (our modern-day major scale), **Dorian**, **Phrygian**, **Lydian**, **Mixolydian**, **Aeolian** (our modern-day natural minor scale), and **Locrian**.

The Ionian mode's arrangement of half steps and whole steps is: 1,1,1/2,1,1,1,1/2.

Ionian Mode

The Dorian mode's construction is: 1,1/2,1,1,1,1/2,1.

Dorian Mode

The Phrygian mode's construction is: 1/2,1,1,1,1/2,1,1.

Phrygian Mode

The Lydian mode's construction is: 1,1,1,1/2,1,1,1/2.

Lydian Mode

The Mixolydian mode's construction is: 1,1,1/2,1,1,1/2,1.

Mixolydian Mode

The Aeolian mode's construction is: 1,1/2,1,1,1/2,1,1.

Aeolian Mode

The Locrian mode's construction is: 1/2,1,1,1/2,1,1,1.

Locrian Mode

A mode can be produced on any of the existing twelve notes using these construction formulas.

The Ionian mode has over the years become the mode of choice because of its inherent stability and stronger sense of unity; thus, through the process of musical evolution, the other modes have passed into relative oblivion. This does not, however, imply that the other modes should be ignored completely. They are of importance and can be drawn from when the musical situation dictates.

Scales Used as Tonal Centers

MAJOR SCALES The Ionian mode has become our *modern* **major scale**. Its arrangement of half steps and whole steps (1,1,1/2,1,1,1,1/2,) can be constructed on any of the twelve existing pitches.

C Major Scale

Db Major Scale

D Major Scale

Eb Major Scale

E Major Scale

F Major Scale

F♯ Major Scale

G♭ Major Scale

G Major Scale

A♭ Major Scale

A Major Scale

B♭ Major Scale

B Major Scale

C♭ Major Scale

C♯ Major Scale

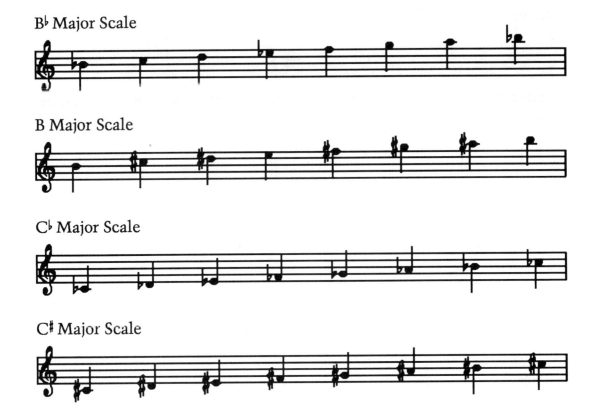

When this is done, we have twelve major keys, each with its own set of *accidentals* accurately marking the intervalic relationship within the scale. When these accidentals are grouped together, *key signatures* are formed.

KEY SIGNATURES

Key signatures sit on a staff immediately following the clef sign. The key signature functions as a code readable by the performer as a means of reducing the number of altered notes within the body of the music to a minimum. The **key signature** tells the performer what notes are to be consistently altered so that only the notes specifically different from the ones within the key signature will appear altered. The arrangement of the accidentals within the key signature is constant but different-looking as the accidentals appear in each clef. These should be memorized in a manner that will indicate both how many accidentals are within the key signature of a major or minor key and how they are written as well.

C Major / A Minor

G Major / E Minor

D Major / B Minor

A Major / F♯ Minor

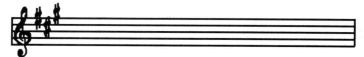

E Major / C♯ Minor

B Major / G♯ Minor

F♯ Major / D♯ Minor

C♯ Major / A♯ Minor

F Major / D Minor

B♭ Major / G Minor

E♭ Major / C Minor

A♭ Major / F Minor

D♭ Major / B♭ Minor

G♭ Major / E♭ Minor

C♭ Major / A♭ Minor

MINOR SCALES   The Aeolian mode's arrangement of half steps and whole steps has become known as the **natural minor scale.** When natural minor scales are constructed on each of the existing twelve pitches, accidentals are again present in order to maintain the integrity of the intervalic relationships. Each natural minor scale has its corresponding key signature. Those minor keys which share the same key signature as a major key are considered relative to one another.

A Natural Minor Scale

E Natural Minor Scale

B Natural Minor Scale

F♯ Natural Minor Scale

C♯ Natural Minor Scale

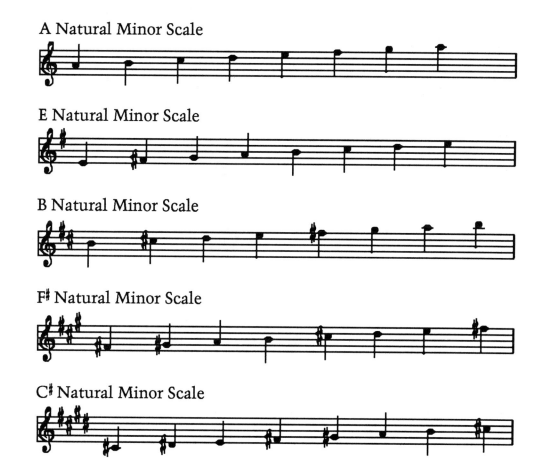

G♯ Natural Minor Scale

D♯ Natural Minor Scale

A♯ Natural Minor Scale

D Natural Minor Scale

G Natural Minor Scale

C Natural Minor Scale

F Natural Minor Scale

B♭ Natural Minor Scale

E♭ Natural Minor Scale

A♭ Natural Minor Scale

The minor keys have two other possible scale arrangements: the **harmonic minor scale** and the **melodic minor scale**. These occur from a tradition of *musica ficta* in earlier practice, whereby notes within a mode were altered to create a half step between the seventh degree of the minor mode and its octave repetition, instead of a whole step. This practice created a *leading tone* within the natural minor scale, which was deemed more satisfactory. This raising of the seventh degree of the natural minor scale became known as the **harmonic minor scale.**

A Harmonic Minor Scale

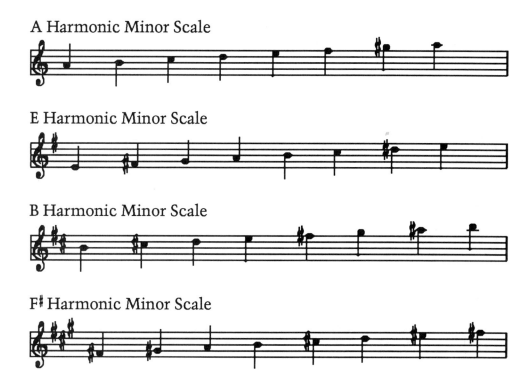

E Harmonic Minor Scale

B Harmonic Minor Scale

F♯ Harmonic Minor Scale

C# Harmonic Minor Scale

G# Harmonic Minor Scale

D# Harmonic Minor Scale

A# Harmonic Minor Scale

D Harmonic Minor Scale

G Harmonic Minor Scale

C Harmonic Minor Scale

F Harmonic Minor Scale

B♭ Harmonic Minor Scale

E♭ Harmonic Minor Scale

A♭ Harmonic Minor Scale

Also, there existed a practice of raising the sixth and seventh degrees of the natural minor scale for expanded melodic possibilities. In actual melodic usage, the composer had the option of either the lowered or raised sixth-scale degree and the raised or lowered seventh-scale degree. When the raised sixth- and seventh-scale degrees were used, it was referred to as the **melodic minor scale.**

A Melodic Minor Scale

E Melodic Minor Scale

B Melodic Minor Scale

F# Melodic Minor Scale

C# Melodic Minor Scale

G# Melodic Minor Scale

D# Melodic Minor Scale

A# Melodic Minor Scale

D Melodic Minor Scale

G Melodic Minor Scale

C Melodic Minor Scale

F Melodic Minor Scale

B♭ Melodic Minor Scale

E♭ Melodic Minor Scale

A♭ Melodic Minor Scale

The natural minor scale, the harmonic minor scale, and the melodic minor scales are all regularly seen within a piece of music in the minor mode. The harmonic form of the scale is most often used to derive chord spelling, while the melodic minor scale is used for the development of melodic material in that it provides

more options within the key. All forms of the three scales may be
used for the creation of melody or harmony, however.

OTHER SCALES
There are other existing scales that can be used for melodic and
harmonic departure points. These may be used in association with
a major or minor tonality or they may be used in isolation, for
their own intrinsic and exotic values.

The **pentatonic scale**, or five-note scale, possesses an Eastern,
Oriental, or African quality. There are two forms of the pentatonic
scale, the **major pentatonic** and the **minor pentatonic**. The major
pentatonic has as its intervalic construction: 1,1,1, minor third, 1;
the minor pentatonic has an arrangement of: minor third, 1,1,
minor third, 1. These scales may be transposed or inverted and
have huge melodic possibilities.

C Major Pentatonic Scale

C Minor Pentatonic Scale

Another scale that has unique qualities is the **whole-tone
scale**. This scale is created with a succession of whole steps. It has
an open feeling associated with it and can create dramatic effects
when melodies are derived from it. Harmonic implications, too,
can be impressive.

C Whole-Tone Scale

There exist two forms of a **diminished scale**. Both types of scales
have a symmetrical content with regard to their construction; they

alternate between whole steps and half steps. They differentiate only with regard to which interval is found first. These scales are sometimes referred to as the **half-step, whole-step scale**, and the **whole-step, half-step scale**. These scales are found almost always in relation to melodic usage.

C Diminished / Whole-Step, Half-Step Scale

C Diminished / Half-Step, Whole-Step Scale

PROJECTS

1. Construct an Ionian, Dorian, Phrygian, Lydian, Mixolydian, Aeolian, and Locrian mode on the note F.

2. Transpose your modes created in Project 1 to all twelve existing pitches.

3. Write all twelve of the major key signatures in both treble and bass clefs.

4. Write all twelve of the minor key signatures in both treble and bass clefs.

5. Construct a whole-tone scale on each of the twelve existing pitches.

6. Construct a major pentatonic scale on each of the twelve existing pitches.

7. Construct a minor pentatonic scale on each of the twelve existing pitches.

8. Construct a half-step, whole-step diminished scale on each of the twelve existing pitches.

9. Construct a whole-step, half-step diminished scale on each of the twelve existing pitches.

3
Chord Spelling

All mainstream popular music in the United States is built on the interval of a third. Our basic unit is the **triad**, a chord that includes two thirds vertically "stacked" above any note. To begin to understand and master chord spelling, one must understand the process of chord construction.

Numbering Notes

When major or minor scales are properly arranged in their order of half steps and whole steps, we may take every note of each scale and build a chord. Each note of the scale then will serve as a *root*. For ease in understanding the process, number each note of the major scale using a Roman numeral as shown on page 27. Use a large Roman numeral to indicate a major triad, a small Roman numeral for a minor triad, a small Roman numeral with a superscript "o" (vii°) for a diminished triad, and a large Roman numeral with a superscript "+" (III+) for an augmented triad. Each chord may be called by either its Roman numeral or its root name.

C-Major Scale

C-Natural Minor Scale

C-Harmonic Minor Scale

C-Melodic Minor Scale

Constructing Triads

To construct a triad, simply skip the *adjacent* note of the scale (in ascending order) and "stack" the *next* note on top of the root. From here, skip the next note of the scale again and "stack" the next scale member onto the two as shown in the following scale. Repeat this process until every scale member has a triad built upon it.

C Major Scale and Chord Construction

I   ii   iii   IV   V   vi   vii°

C Natural Minor Scale

i   ii°   III   iv   v   VI   VII

C Harmonic Minor Scale

i   ii°   III⁺   iv   V   VI   vii°

C Ascending Melodic Minor Scale

i   ii   III⁺   IV   V   vi°   vii°

Once triads have been created from the major scale, names are given to each member of the triad. The lowest note in the chord, or the scale member upon which the chord is built, is called the **root.** The next note up from the root is called the **third** because the interval is a third away from the root. The top note of the triad is called the **fifth** because it is an interval of a fifth away from the root.

Root 3rd   5th

Types of Triads

All triads are not the same in regard to their sound or quality. Some triads are **major**, while some are **minor**, **diminished**, or **augmented**. This distinction has to do with the quality of intervals that make up the triad. In a major triad, the *distance* from the root to the third of the chord will be a **major third** interval. Within the same chord the *distance* from the root to the fifth will be a **Perfect fifth** interval.

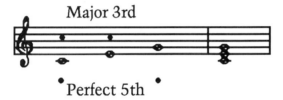

In a **minor triad** the intervallic relationships are different. The distance from the root to the third is a **minor third** interval, while the distance from the root to the fifth remains a Perfect fifth.

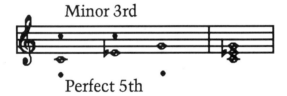

A **diminished triad** contains a minor third and a diminished fifth interval from the root.

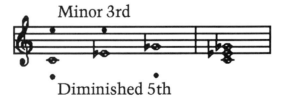

Also, an **augmented triad** contains the intervals of a major third and an augmented fifth up from the root of the chord.

Major 3rd

Augmented 5th

Diatonic Chords

These "quality" distinctions of chords, major triad, minor triad, etc., are not contrived, but naturally occur during chord construction due to the nature of the whole steps and half steps found in the major scale from which the chords are built. When triads are constructed from any major scale, these quality distinctions will remain constant. The I, IV, and V chords will be major triads, whereas the ii, iii, and vi chords will be minor. The vii° chord is diminished in quality. Because these quality distinctions occur naturally, without any manipulation of intervals, we refer to these chords as being **diatonic**.

C Major Scale

I   ii   iii   IV   V   vi   vii°

When triads are constructed from the natural minor scale, these diatonic quality distinctions will remain constant. The i, iv, and v chords will be minor triads, while the III, VI, and VII chords will be major triads. The ii° chord will be a diminished triad.

C Natural Minor Scale

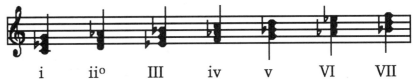

i   ii°   III   iv   v   VI   VII

When triads are constructed from the harmonic minor scale, these diatonic quality distinctions will remain constant. The i and iv chords will be minor triads, the V and VI chords will be major triads, whereas the ii° and vii° chords are diminished triads. The III⁺ chord will be augmented.

C Harmonic Minor Scale

i   ii°   III⁺   iv   V   VI   vii°

PROJECTS

1. Create triads on each note of all twelve major keys.

2. Give each chord of the keys you've chosen a Roman numeral.

3. Make a game out of chord spelling by referring to a chord's Roman numeral and trying to spell that chord. (*Example*: The IV chord in F major is _____.)

4. Repeat the game until you can spell any of the chords I through vii in any of the twelve major keys.

5. Repeat Projects 1 through 4 for all twelve of the minor keys using the natural minor form of the scale.

6. Repeat Projects 1 through 4 for all twelve minor keys using the harmonic minor form of the scale.

4

Seventh Chords

A **seventh chord**, a four-note chord in which the interval of a seventh is "stacked" on top of the triad, may be constructed in the same manner in which triads were built. The adjacent note of the scale is skipped, past the fifth of the triad, and the next scale degree is placed onto the triad creating a four-note seventh chord.

7th Chords Built on C Major Scale

Seventh Intervals

When seventh chords are built on each member of the major or minor scales, the Roman numerals associated with the chords have to indicate the presence of the seventh interval as well. This is accomplished by the addition of a raised "7" next to the Roman numeral of each chord.

C Major Scale

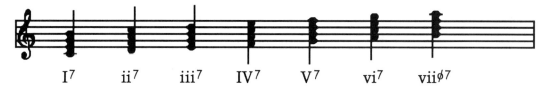

$$\text{I}^7 \quad \text{ii}^7 \quad \text{iii}^7 \quad \text{IV}^7 \quad \text{V}^7 \quad \text{vi}^7 \quad \text{vii}^{\varnothing 7}$$

7th Chords Built on C Natural Minor Scale

$$\text{i}^7 \quad \text{ii}^{\varnothing 7} \quad \text{III}^7 \quad \text{iv}^7 \quad \text{v}^7 \quad \text{VI}^7 \quad \text{VII}^7$$

7th Chords Built on C Harmonic Minor Scale

$$i^7 \quad ii^{\o7} \quad III^{+7} \quad iv^7 \quad V^7 \quad VI^7 \quad vii^{o7}$$

All seventh intervals are not the same with regard to their "quality." When constructing a seventh chord from a major scale that possesses a certain arrangement of whole steps and half steps, the intervals between the root and the seventh of the chord will differ. In the I^7 and the IV^7 chords, the interval between the root and seventh will be a major seventh interval. In the ii^7, iii^7, V^7, and vi^7 chords, the interval between the root and seventh of each chord will be a minor seventh interval. The $vii^{\o7}$ is considered to be **half-diminished**, meaning that a *minor seventh interval* has been added to a *diminished triad*. When a *diminished seventh interval* is added to a *diminished triad*, it is considered to be a **fully diminished seventh chord,** as is the case with vii^{o7} in a minor key using the harmonic form of the minor scale.

In the case of the **harmonic minor** scale, i^7, $ii^{\o7}$, iv^7, and V^7 will possess minor 7th intervals from the root of each chord. III^{+7} and VI^7 will possess major 7th intervals from the root of their chords. In the case of the **natural minor** scale being used to build 7th chords, all of the 7th intervals will remain the same as they appear in the harmonic form of the minor scale; the root of the of the VII chord is a half step lower, however.

Seventh chords possess a richer color than do triads and can be used in place of triads at will; however, it is best to stay consistent in the choice of basic chord unit for a piece of music. An exception is when the triad is chosen as the basic unit for harmonic construction; then the V^7 is routinely inserted.

PROJECTS

1. Create seventh chords on each scale member in the key of C major. Make sure to include Roman numerals below each chord in the sequence.

2. Create similar seventh chords for each scale member in all twelve major keys.

3. Isolate the ii^7 chord and spell it in all twelve major keys.

4. Do the same for iii^7, IV^7, V^7, vi^7, and vii^7.

5. Repeat projects 2 through 4 and apply them to all twelve minor keys using the harmonic form of the scale.

6. Repeat projects 2 through 4 and apply them to all twelve minor keys using the natural minor form of the scale.

Part Two
Harmony

5
Chord Functions

Harmonic motion, which describes how music moves throughout a key area, can be thought of as similar to the dynamics of an automobile engine. In a car engine, fuel is the explosive ingredient that is put under pressure by pistons and is ignited by the spark of a spark plug. This ignition of the fuel creates a miniexplosion that forces the pistons out, down the cylinder chamber. These pistons are then attached to a rod that makes the car move. The same thing happens in music.

Intervals and Harmonic Motion

Harmonic motion is created through intervals and their inherent stability or instability. When intervals are "stacked," as they are in chords, the intervals that make up the chords react to one another. All the intervals in the chords of the diatonic chord sequence range from very stable, like the I chord, to relatively stable, like the IV chord, to very unstable, as in having the tendency to "lean" or move as in the case of the V^7 or vii° chord.

The instability is primarily caused by the presence of the unstable **tritone,** the augmented fourth or diminished fifth interval. In the case of the V⁷, the interval between the third of the chord and the seventh of the chord is a tritone. This tritone wants to collapse in on itself to a more stable interval of a third. This "collapsing" is what makes V⁷ "move" to the I chord, whose intervals include the third to which the tritone resolves.

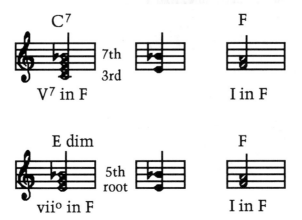

When chords are constructed upon members of any scale, whether the chords are triads or seventh chords, each chord will serve the tonal motion in a different capacity.

Tonic

Tonic, or the I chord, is at rest or "home." There is no need to move, for it possesses a strong Perfect fifth interval between the root and the fifth. A major third is also present between the root and the third, and a minor third between the third and the fifth of the chord. The iii chord can be considered as an extension of the I chord and will function as a substitute for I.

I Chord in F Major

iii⁷ Chord in F Major

Dominant

Dominant, or primarily the V chord, is very unstable and wants to "move" to tonic or "home." The V triad possesses the *leading tone*, the seventh degree of the scale appearing as the third of the chord. This third wants to "rise" to the tonic note of the key, thus creating the V or vii chord's aural role of returning "home" to tonic. If the V chord appears as V⁷, the leading tone is present as the third of the chord; but an interval of a tritone also exists between the third of the chord and the seventh of the chord, making the V⁷ chord even more unstable and in need of resolution.

V⁷ Chord in F Major

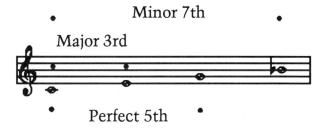

vii∅⁷ in F Major

The vii chord and V chord are as one in the dominant-function category. They possess the same qualities and are therefore substitutes for each other.

Subdominant

Subdominant, or the "traveling" group of chords, contain the ii chord and the IV chord. The IV chord is an extension of the ii chord, or vice versa, within the subdominant group. These chords "travel" back and forth to tonic function chords or to dominant function chords. They possess strong interval combinations such as the Perfect fifth and the major third, up from the root of the chord, and contain no leading tones or tritones in either their triad appearance or their seventh-chord appearance.

IV^7 in F Major

ii^7 in F Major

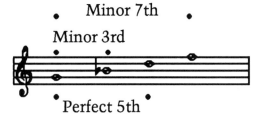

Chord Function Table

TONIC	SUBDOMINANT	DOMINANT
(Home)	(Traveling)	(Going Home)
I, i	ii, ii°	V, v
iii, III	IV, iv	vii°, VII
(vi, VI)	(vi, VI)	

PROJECTS

1. Spell the tonic-function chord possibilities of all twelve major keys.

2. Spell the tonic-function chord possibilities of all twelve minor keys.

3. Spell the subdominant-function chord possibilities of all twelve major keys.

4. Spell the subdominant-function chord possibilities of all twelve minor keys.

5. Spell the dominant-function chord possibilities of all twelve major keys.

6. Spell the dominant-function chord possibilities of all twelve minor keys.

6
Chord Extensions

Chords may be *extended* to include chord members beyond the seventh. This is accomplished by repeating the process of "stacking" of thirds on top of the seventh of the chord. When this process is completed, the addition of the **ninth, eleventh,** and **thirteenth** will appear. If a chord uses all the diatonic extensions, the root through the thirteenth, all seven scale members will be present.

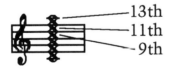

Chord-Symbol Notation

When extensions are to be used, the chord-symbol notation will indicate a letter name and a numerical inclusion. If the number, indicating interval from the root of the chord, is outside parentheses, the interval indicated is diatonic. When an interval that has been diatonically altered is to be a chord member, the corresponding number of the interval and its alteration indication will appear within parentheses.

C^{13}

$C^{13}\left(\begin{smallmatrix}\flat 9\\ \sharp 5\end{smallmatrix}\right)$

Use of Ninths

When the ninth is employed, it may be used in three ways. The ninth of the chord may appear in its diatonic state, 9, or altered up or down by a half step creating a ♯9 or a ♭9. Both the ♯9 and the ♭9 may be present either together or separately, but never in conjunction with the regular ninth. If the regular ninth appears with an altered ninth, these notes will be a half step apart, creating an unacceptable "grind."

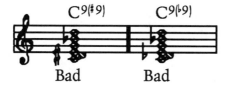

The addition of the ninth may appear on a major seventh chord, minor seventh chord, or dominant seventh chord, (V⁷). If the ninth is used on the major seventh chord, it will appear as a diatonic ninth, with no alteration. If it appears in a minor seventh chord, it will be a diatonic ninth as well. If the ninth is used in conjunction with a dominant seventh chord, the ninth may appear diatonically or in its altered state.

The ninth may appear in a chord without the presence of the seventh. In this case the chord will indicate C⁽ᵃᵈᵈ ⁹⁾, or C⁽ᵃᵈᵈ ²⁾. This will be the addition of the diatonic ninth, unaltered.

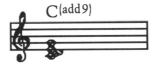

Use of Elevenths

In a **major seventh** or **dominant seventh chord**, the diatonic eleventh will be only a half step away from the third of the chord. This creates a confusing "grind" because the diatonic eleventh on these chords acts as a suspended third; thus, the suspended third and the regular third are both present. To avoid having a suspended third present with a regular third when the eleventh is employed, the eleventh is raised by a half step creating a sharped eleventh. When the eleventh is raised, the distance between the third of the chord and the eleventh will be a whole step.

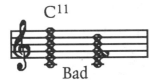

$Cma^{9(\sharp 11)}$

Occasionally, you will see in published sheet music C^{11}, seemingly a major triad with the addition of the eleventh. What is erroneously being indicated with this symbol is a C^{sus} chord, where the third is suspended and is not actually present.

On **minor triads** the third of the chord is already lowered; thus, the presence of the eleventh diatonically will be a whole step. The sound of the eleventh on a minor seventh chord is acceptable.

Cmi^{11} $Cmi^{11(ma7)}$ $Cmi^{(addF)}$ or $Cmi^{(add11)}$ $Cmi\binom{ma7}{ma11}$

$Cmi^{7(add11)}$

As extensions are placed above a seventh chord, the higher the number of the extension, the lower the extension that is implied to be present. *Example*: If a minor eleventh chord were to be indicated, the ninth and seventh would be assumed to be included, even though the chord symbol would only indicate $Dmin^{11}$. If the eleventh were desired without the ninth, it would appear in the chord symbol $Dmin^{7(add11)}$ or $D^{7(add\sharp 11)}$. Sometimes the note name itself is indicated in parentheses without using a numeral association, $Cmin^{(addF)}$.

Alterations of Fifths

The fifth interval may be altered up or down by a half step. This alteration will occur only on chords possessing a dominant seventh interval. As with the ninth, either the flatted fifth or sharped fifth intervals may be used separately or sounding together, but never in conjunction with the diatonic fifth. Also, if an alteration of the fifth is to occur, it will be indicated within parentheses.

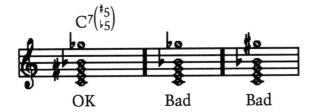

The flatted fifth interval is an **enharmonic** spelling (same pitch, different spelling) of the sharped eleventh interval.

Use of Thirteenths

Thirteenths will appear much like ninths. The diatonic thirteenth is used in major seventh chords and minor seventh chords. As with ninths and elevenths, if a thirteenth is indicated in the chord symbol and this is the only numeral indicated, the ninth and seventh are implied. The thirteenth on a minor seventh chord will imply the inclusion of the eleventh as well, whereas the thirteenth on a major seventh or dominant seventh chord implies only the ninth and seventh. The eleventh on a major seventh chord or dominant seventh chord, as has been stated earlier, will be separated in parentheses because of its raised or altered status.

Thirteenths, too, may be altered up or down by a half step. In actual usage, the raised thirteenth is the minor seventh interval on a dominant chord enharmonically spelled and is therefore redundant and never indicated. The flat thirteenth is also an enharmonic spelling of the ♯5th interval, but is occasionally indicated when a melodic passage passes from the diatonic thirteenth, through the flat thirteenth, before resolving to the diatonic fifth of the chord or to any other chord member, if the harmony changes. If the flat thirteenth is to be used as a chord member without a melodic passing motion first starting on the diatonic thirteenth, it is indicated as (♯5) instead of (♭13).

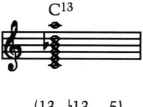

As with ninths and elevenths, when a thirteenth is to be included as a chord member on a **major seventh** chord or **minor seventh** chord, the thirteenth interval will be diatonic and unaltered. *The chromatic alterations of any fifth, ninth, or thirteenth interval will occur only on dominant chords.*

The $\frac{9}{6}$ Chord

In the big-band era, a triad was considered too bland to use, and so the sixth-scale degree was added to the triad, C⁶. This inclusion was more satisfactory and was commonly used on any nondominant chord, **major** or **minor**, C^6 or Cmi^6. As has been indicated previously, the addition of the ninth may also be placed on the triad. When both the sixth and ninth are added to a triad without the presence of a seventh, it is referred to as a $\frac{9}{6}$ or $\frac{6}{9}$ chord. This inclusion is found on both major and minor triads.

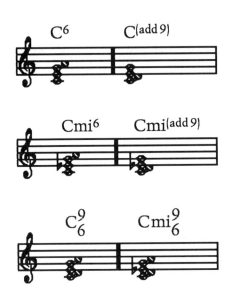

PROJECTS

1. Spell an F major thirteenth chord.

2. Spell an F minor thirteenth chord.

3. Spell an F^{13} chord.

4. Spell an F^{13} $\begin{pmatrix} \flat 9, \sharp 9 \\ \sharp 11 \\ \sharp 5 \end{pmatrix}$ chord.

5. Spell an F^6 chord.

6. Spell an F$^9_6$ chord.

7. Spell an F$^{(add\ 9)}$ chord.

8. Transpose projects 1–7 to all twelve chromatic notes and spell those chords.

7

Chord Voicings

Once the form, melodies, countermelodies, and chord progressions have been established, the decisions of *chord voicings* may be approached. **Chord voicings**, or the *arrangement of intervals between chord members*, can add substantially to the character, mood, and quality of the harmonic progression that has been chosen. There are several standard techniques to choose from with regard to chord voicing. Each possesses a quality that is unique and useful in itself. There should be experimentation in chord voicings so as to achieve the right sound for the music. The same voicing will not work in all types of music, so it is best to be able to pick and choose which type of voicing is most effective.

Closed/Open Position

Closed position is a term referring to a chord *spelled in thirds*, with no extra space between chord members.

Open position is a term refer-ring to a chord in which the arrangement of the chord mem-bers *occupies a wider space than the "stacked" closed-posi-tion voicing.*

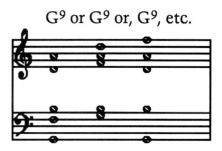

G⁹ or G⁹ or, G⁹, etc.

These terms, closed or open position, are generic in nature and can refer to any voicing that fits within the definition.

Closed Position	Open Position
"Stacked" or root posi-tion chord spelling	Drop 2
	Drop 2 and 4
Clusters	Quartal

Drop 2

The **drop 2** voicing is an open voicing in which the arrangement begins with the closed-position voicing of a chord. If a chord is voiced in closed position and its chord members are assigned a number from the soprano voice descending to the bass voice, the drop 2 voicing would "DROP ♯2," one octave.

Fma⁹/Closed to Fma⁹/Drop 2

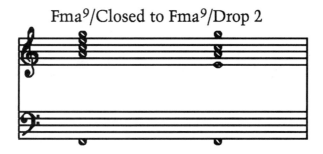

The drop 2 voicing provides a feeling of openness and warmth and gets away from the sterile closed position of "stacked thirds." This technique also allows the melody note ample space without being "crowded."

Drop 2 and 4

Like the drop 2 voicing, **drop 2 and 4** is literally dropping the second and fourth chord members from the soprano voice of the closed-position chord down one octave.

Fma⁹/Closed to Fma⁹/Drop 2/4

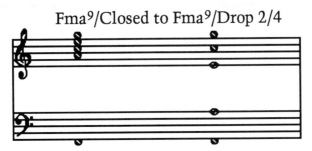

The drop 2 and 4 has a different quality from the drop 2 or the closed-position voicings, lending more possibilities in color.

Quartal/4th Voicings

A **quartal voicing** is a voicing in which the chord members are arranged in stacks of fourth intervals. Usually, there are only three chord members selected to be "stacked" in fourths. The root of the chord is rarely seen when this voicing is used. The quartal voicing has a strident quality and can be very powerful when played by the piano, brass, vibes, or strings.

Cma¹³

This voicing concept also works well with a combination of fourths and thirds. When there is an incorporation of third intervals and fourth intervals, more chord members are able to be included.

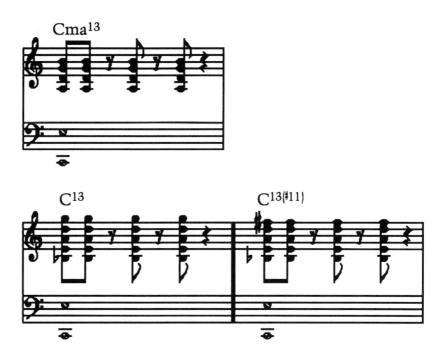

Clusters

Clusters is a term associated with a chord voicing that is extremely "tight" or in a closer arrangement than the normal closed-position voicing. The cluster voicing occurs within the span of an octave and can possess any number of chord members, while the root need not be present. The cluster voicing creates an extremely strident and "biting" quality that may be used with both up-tempo tunes and ballads.

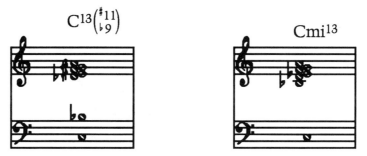

"Clusters" may be created from scales as well as from chords. A cluster can be made from the whole-tone scale, the diminished scale, or from just a "handful" of half steps. These techniques can provide an array of "special effects" when used as **"pads,"** that is, background support material.

Other Open-Position Voicings

Voicings can be created in any manner that is desired; however, some ways are more useful and successful than others. There are some rules of thumb that may be helpful in experimentation with voicings. These are:

1. The interval of a tenth from the root, if in root position, is a satisfactory spacing on which to build a voicing.

    Almost anything sitting on top of a tenth interval will work.

2. The interval of a seventh in the bass works well.

    A seventh interval in the bass is almost as strong as a tenth.

3. Avoid muddiness. Do not get too low in the registers. Thirds between the bass and the next chord member become muddy when the bass reaches around F^2. At this point, switch to another interval between the bass and the next chord member in the voicing.

, etc.

4. The inclusion of the Perfect fifth above the root in the bass before the next chord member in the voicing can have a heroic or military sound. At the very least, it adds power to the voicing.

PROJECTS

1. Spell the $C^{13(\sharp11)}$ chord in closed position.

2. Spell the same chord in any open position.

3. Spell the same chord using a drop 2 voicing.

4. Spell the same chord using a drop 2 and 4 voicing.

5. Spell a C^{9}_{6} chord in a quartal voicing without the root.

6. Spell a $C^{13(\sharp11)}$ chord using a mixture of fourths and thirds.

7. Spell the same chord in a cluster voicing.

8. Create at least two other voicings of the same chord using some of the techniques suggested in the section on *other open voicings*.

9. Transpose projects 1–8 using all twelve pitches as roots.

8
Voice Leading

Acquiring knowledge of musical form, harmonic structure, style, and psychological implications does little good without the proper understanding and mastery of *voice leading*. The term **voice leading** implies a melody derived from chord members. These small melodies may be of lesser consideration and focus than the primary or secondary melodies, but they are perceived as miniature melodies nonetheless. The aural perception and reaction to chord-member resolution is as keen as any other portion of musical awareness.

Movement from Chord to Chord

The principles of voice leading in commercial or popular music have not changed to a great extent from those that governed this music in previous eras. There is one prime directive that is important to keep in mind when "voices" move and resolve from chord to chord: *keep common tones and move as stepwise as possible.* This basic principle, if followed, will solve most voice-leading problems. This basically means that if there are common tones from one chord to the next, keep those tones in the same voice. If there are voices that have to be resolved other than those common tones, move to a resolution in as stepwise a fashion as possible. This motion will create a smooth flow from voice to voice and will avoid large unnecessary skips or awkward leaps that draw the listener's ear to the awkward movement.

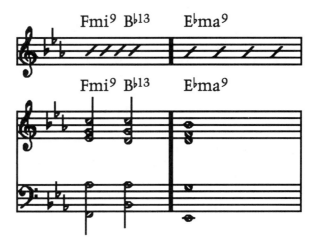

Every voicing, whether functioning as a background "pad" or secondary horn "shots," or string countermelody, or the primary melodic material of a particular musical section, will possess a melodic line. The other notes within the voicing will function as color enhancers for that melodic line. Therefore, when part-writing these voicings, keep the melody in the same voice so that it does not weave in and out of inner voices, muddying the aural awareness of its presence.

Guide Tones

When any ii-V chord progression is used, there will appear standard guide tones that should be resolved correctly, enhancing the richness of the material within a musical passage. If the primary "rule of thumb" for voice leading is followed, keep common tones and move as stepwise as possible; these guide tones will already have been part-written correctly.

The guide tones have a ranking of importance. The **primary guide tones are the third and seventh** of any chord (if seventh chords are being used as the base of the harmonic language color). In a ii-V sequence, the primary guide tones will "flip-flop" in chord function. As an example, the guide tones of the chord progression Dmi⁷ to G⁷ would be: F for the third and C for the seventh of the Dmi⁷ chord; F for the seventh and B for the third of the G⁷ chord. If part-written correctly, the third of the Dmi⁷ chord, F, will become the seventh of the G⁷ chord and should remain in the same voice that it appears in the Dmi⁷ chord. The seventh of the Dmi⁷ chord, C, should resolve to the third of the G⁷ chord, B, down by a step.

When a chain of ii-V's is present, the primary guide tones can be easily discernible aurally by their common tone and downward resolution by a step.

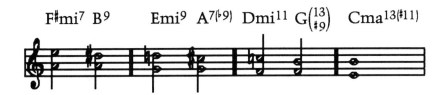

Regardless of how many voices are used, the primary guide tones should be present within the chord voicing. The primary guide tones give the essential sound quality to the chord, whether the root of the chord is present within the voicing or not. Even if the number of voices within the chord is only three, the primary guide tones, the third and seventh of the chord, should be present.

Secondary guide tones include the fifth of the chord and the ninth of the chord in a ii-V progression. These too will "flip-flop" with the fifth of the ii chord becoming the ninth of the V chord and retained in the same voice, while the ninth of the ii chord will resolve by step to the fifth of the V chord.

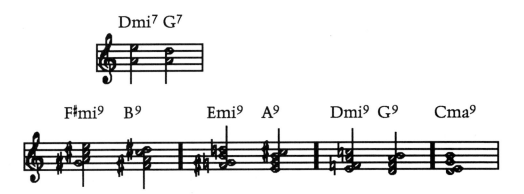

Movement within the Same Chord

When melodies occur over one chord, there will appear chord members and possibly nonharmonic tones. If the melody moves from chord member to chord member by a small skip, simple inversions of the chord, moving as smoothly as possible, will suffice for part-writing purposes.

If the melody leaps over a wider interval from chord member to chord member, the original voicing may choose to widen to a more open voicing in order to cover the space created by the melodic leap more smoothly. The inversion motion of the voices should be as smooth as possible.

If the melody to be part-written passes through nonharmonic tones, choices of harmonization can be varied, but the voice-leading principle will remain the same; keep common tones, if any, and move as stepwise as possible. If the melodic movement is small, the same voicing is used. If the melody leaps, a spreading of the voicing may be most effective to cover the span created by the melodic leap.

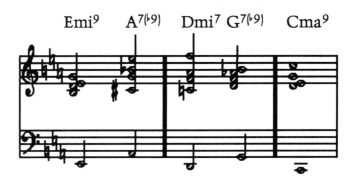

PROJECTS

1. Part-write the chord progression iii^7-vi^7-ii^7-V^7-I^7 in C major using a four-note voicing. Identify the primary guide tones.

2. Transpose the progression written in project 1 to all twelve major keys.

3. Use the same progression in project 1 and part-write using a five-note voicing. Include primary and secondary guide tones within each chord.

4. Transpose project 3 to all twelve major keys.

9

Modulations

The concept of modulation is the process of changing keys through the canceling of one leading tone and the inserting of another. Changing keys need not be confusing. Knowing what key to change to and how to modulate from one key to another are the necessary skills of a composer and/or arranger.

Why Isn't Everything in C Major?

The key in which you write or play acts as the home base for the composition or arrangement. The choice of key is a necessary decision that has to be made from the beginning. Factors that go into the choice of key can be as easy as, "my singer sounds best in this key," or "the trombone is playing the lead in the bridge." These are valid considerations for the need to be in a certain key either for the whole tune or a portion of that tune, based on the range of the instruments used. This is primarily an arranging problem. Other considerations might be the psychological or mood implications of any key.

Keys have traditionally had moods associated with them. As one goes around the cycle of fifths, each key area is not aesthetically the same. There has been the belief that each key represents its own psychological feeling, mood, or color. Traditionally, C major is calm, while the sharp keys have graded shadings of brightness associated with them as more sharps are added to the key signature. The flat keys are somber and also progress in darkness or heaviness as more flats appear in the key signature.

These mood aspects are only speculative at best and there are no written rules for present-day use. There has always been some validity to this concept and some experimentation on the part of the composer or arranger could serve your piece well in its overall effect when you pick an initial key.

Which Key Should I Go To?

The need to change key is an obvious one. By its nature, your music is dependent on the dimension of time. Interest has to be created in this dimension. During the earlier eras of composition, composers from Bach to Beethoven to Mahler used *form* as a guiding force that determined the key relationships. Form is the architecture on which a piece of music is structured. These composers were greatly skilled at the development of an idea or set of ideas. They employed forms that made use of key relationships as a primary catalyst for the development of musical interest during their compositions. The keys that were most chosen to modulate to or from were primarily based on the *cycle of fifths*.

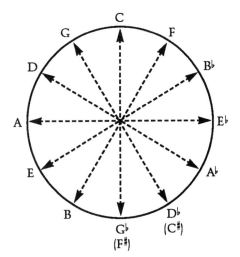

The cycle of fifths determines closely related keys and distantly related keys. This is determined by moving forward or backward from your chosen key, as it is found on the circle. By moving forward, you add an accidental; by moving backward, you subtract one.

Another practice of traditional composers was to modulate to a relative major or minor key. The **relative minor key** is the minor key that shares the same key signature as the corresponding major key, and vice versa. Modulations based upon the circle of fifths and modulations based on relative keys are still valid techniques and provide an aurally smooth and logical movement.

Commercial practices are somewhat different, however. Since the creation and proliferation of the broadcast media, there has been a severe crunch placed on time. Recordings have come to be a certain standard length, due to the broadcaster's hourly play format. This format is determined by how many records can be played in an hour, with the maximum amount of commercial advertising space inserted. The broadcaster's purpose is not primarily to present the most and best music to the public. It is to attract and keep as large a target audience as possible, while keeping that audience entertained and interested so that they will continue to listen to the station. In this way the maximum amount of advertising can be broadcast to that audience.

This bold fact is what has shortened commercial music's time element from much longer time frames, which may be beneficial from an artistic standpoint, to roughly 3:30 minutes each, the broadcaster's time frame, and consequently, the audience's conditioned concentration-time limit. This shortened time constraint applies to video and film, as well as to television. Only in a live concert setting, where the audience pays to hear the music, is there more time to be artistically and psychologically creative.

The time concept affects commercial music in that the composer, the arranger, or the artist wants the maximum amount of satisfying effect in the least amount of time when it comes to key changes. Thus, we have the problem of creating musical interest in a short time span.

This dilemma has forced the commercial artist to rely on the "Broadway" modulation most often. Broadway modulation raises the key of the piece by a half step or a whole step, depending on the taste of the artist, to produce a rising effect or one of heightened interest emotionally. This is not a key relationship-based modulation, but a psychologically based decision. Broadway modulation creates musical interest; also, it gives the music a lift at just the right time to avoid boredom.

Recording artists have the curse of being tied to the record. The recording is what is presented to the public first, what creates the initial acceptance by the public, and what is psychologically reinforced by its repetition on the consumer's stereo equipment when purchased. When the artist performs for the public in a concert situation, the audience has paid to hear live what it already musically accepts from that artist as introduced to it by the media. The artist does not want to run the risk of disappointing that existing audience, so he/she faithfully reproduces live what is on the recording. This vicious cycle of faithful reproduction, based in essence on monetary concerns, has become a commonly accepted musical practice in many aspects of commercial music composition and performance, including modulation techniques.

How Do I Change Keys?

There are three basic ways that modulations occur in popular harmony. These include:

1. The surprise modulation,
2. the V and go modulation, and
3. the prepared modulation.

SURPLISE
MODULATION

The **surprise modulation** is the simplest of the three types. The music comes to the end of a section, *cadences*, and immediately begins the new section in a new key area. This type of key change occurs with no preparation harmonically and no preparation or warning given emotionally. This is why it has a surprising or shocking effect on the listener. The surprise modulation can be used effectively, but can also be overused, diminishing its utility. Use this type of key change sparingly to maximize its effect.

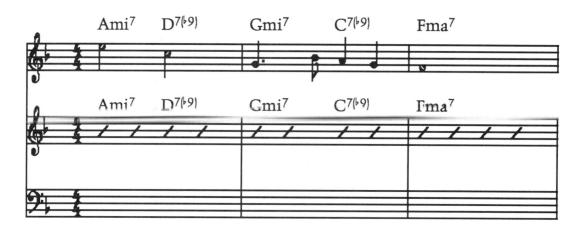

V AND GO The **V and go** type of modulation is the most common. When the area of the piece where the key change is to occur is identified, the *dominant chord* of the key being modulated to is inserted, followed by the *tonic* of the new key. This kind of key change takes up little harmonic rhythm and it is aurally convincing in that the key change has been satisfactorily completed. More dramatic effects can occur with this type of modulation if the dominant chord of the new key is elongated in its rhythm (elongated disproportionately to the piece's regular harmonic rhythm). This calls attention to the new key's dominant chord and builds tension. The more time the tension has to build, the more dramatic will be the emotional release when the new tonic is finally heard.

PREPARED MODULATION The prepared modulation has two types, the **prepared modulation** and the **pivot-chord modulation.** The prepared modulation has included not only the dominant chord of the new key, but a *subdominant chord* in the new key as well. This type of key change is a little rarer than the V and go type because it takes a little more time to set up, but it can be equally satisfying.

To create a prepared modulation, a chain of subdominant and dominant chords of the new key are placed at a cadence point of the piece, before arriving at the new tonic. The subdominant chords can be either ii or IV, with the dominant chord being usually V⁷ or V⁷ suspended (sometimes vii).

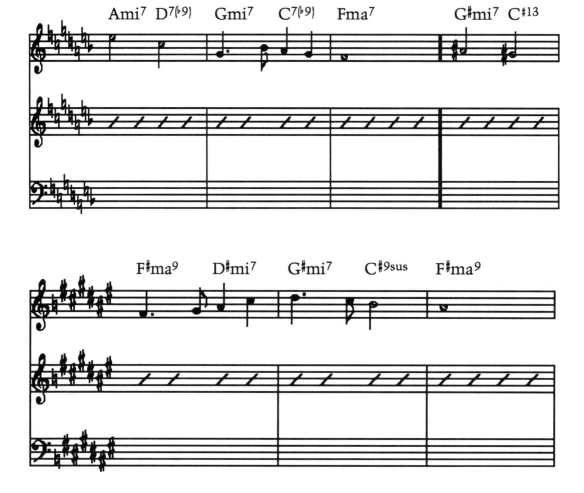

The pivot-chord modulation is very much like the prepared modulation in that it is prepared harmonically through the use of subdominant, dominant, and tonic chords in the new key to give a complete setting up of the change in tonality. It varies in that the subdominant-function chord of the new key is found normally, or diatonically, in the old key, but may be a different function. The A minor triad is diatonically vi in C major, but is ii in G major. Thus, a pivot-chord modulation from the key of C major to G major would use the A minor, vi in C major, and ii in G major as the **pivot** chord or open door that would usher in a smooth and hardly noticeable key change, when followed by G major's dominant chord, D^7, before arriving at the new key's tonic: G major.

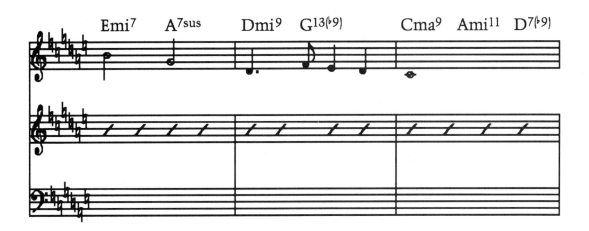

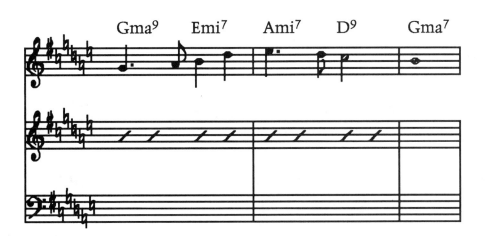

PROJECTS

In Projects 1–10, select an eight-bar section from a piece of music that either you have written or have borrowed from someone else.

1. Transpose the section to C major, if it is not already in this key.

2. Create a key change using the surprise type of modulation from C major to D major.

3. Create a key change using the V and go type of modulation between the same two keys.

4. Create a key change using the prepared modulation (subdominant, dominant, tonic) in the same two keys.

5. Create a key change from C major to G major using the pivot-chord type of modulation.

6. Transpose your original piece of music to all twelve major keys.

7. Create a key change from *each* of the twelve examples of Project 6 *to* A major using first the surprise technique, then the V and go technique, and then the prepared technique.

8. Transpose your original example from C major to C minor.

9. Create a key change from C minor to *all* twelve minor keys using the surprise technique, then the V and go technique, and finally, the prepared technique.

10. Pick from the transposed originals and create a modulation from a major key to a minor key *and vice versa*.

10
Chord Substitution

From the scales that have been diagramed in the previous chapters, one can see that the scale members have been given numbers. Chords, both triads and seventh chords, have been constructed upon these scale members and have been referred to by their numerical name, I chord, vi^7 chord, etc. Functions, such as tonic, dominant, and subdominant, have been applied to each chord within a scale or **tonality.** Subdominant moves to dominant, dominant moves to tonic, tonic is at rest; these are the motion tendencies that have been indicated. With these concepts in mind, we may begin to discuss how the "motor" of popular harmony actually gets set into motion.

Subdominant Chords

The primary usage of the subdominant chords, ii or ii° and IV or iv, in popular harmony depends on the style of music that is portrayed. In historically white music—country, rock, and bluegrass—IV or iv is predominant, while in historically black music—jazz, blues, gospel, and rhythm-and-blues—the use of the ii chord is more prominent. Since the mid-1940s popular music has primarily taken on the influence of black music's harmonic language and this governs the "theoretical tendencies" practiced by the people who created the genre and language. Therefore, *ii or ii° is the preferred subdominant chord.*

Dominant Chords

Popular harmony uses primarily **root-position** harmony, chords that are **voiced** with the root in the bass. The harmonic motion of popular-music harmony is best seen when the bass is isolated for analysis. We therefore will focus on the tendencies of motion centered in the bass voice. But, before beginning to understand harmonic motion, some concepts must be mastered and internalized that will serve as "windows" through which we may peer and begin to see how harmony is manipulated.

Through the principle of **borrowed harmony**, a concept in traditional harmony of "borrowing" a chord from the **parallel major or minor**, *any dominant chord found in major or minor tonality may be used as a substitute for another dominant function chord.*

The dominant chord's root, V or vii, moves to I or i or tonic. This motion is called an **authentic cadential movement**, dominant to tonic. This concept applies primarily to V-I root movement, but may be secondarily considered to include vii-I as well. This remains true regardless of the quality of chord that is built upon that root. The quality of dominant chord and tonic chord will change according to the key in which the music is written, major or minor. Of course, there are three different forms of the minor mode, so this will affect the quality of the dominant and the tonic chords. *Dominant quality chords may be: V or V⁷, v or v⁷, vii, half-diminished vii⁷, fully diminished vii⁷, VII, or VII⁷.*

V   V⁷   I   i   v   v⁷   I   i   vii   vii^{ø7}   vii°⁷

I   i   VII   VII^7 VII^7 I   i

Neapolitan Substitution (Tritone Substitution)

In traditional harmony before the Age of Impressionism, the **Neapolitan chord**, a major triad built on the flat second-scale degree, was a subdominant chord found in second inversion, the fifth of the chord in the bass. In the impressionistic period, as well as the jazz periods of bebop and cool, the Neapolitan chord began to be used as a dominant-function chord and thus as *a substitute for V and vii*. We, therefore, may add the Neapolitan, usually found with its seventh or N^7, to the list of dominant-root possibilities.

N   N^7

N^7 I   i   ii^7 N^7 I^7

ii^7-V^7-I

Through the principle of the **secondary dominant**, a concept also found in traditional harmony, a chord may act like a temporary I chord and may be preceded by its dominant.

The "cycle of fifths" is a useful tool in visualizing many aspects of harmonic motion. This "cycle" is most frequently used to explain key signatures. We may use it to see the ease and logic associated with "substituting" chords.

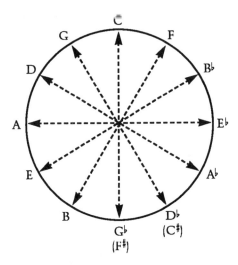

The cycle of fifths works like the clock. The harmonic motion "moves" clockwise with each note serving as "V of . . ." or in a dominant capacity. If we use any one of the notes as our arrival point, or **temporary I chord**, we can see how we would back up from our arrival point to see which chord root will serve as a dominant, or V. If you were to back up, or go counterclockwise, once again from the root of the V chord, the ii chord's root would appear because ii is a fourth away from V. This root is also the root of the secondary dominant, V of V, or V/V.

The preceding example focuses on the root motion of each chord. The quality of the chord "sitting" on top of the root can come from any of the borrowing possibilities previously listed. The choice of chord quality is dependent on the "color" desired and the melody note that is being harmonized.

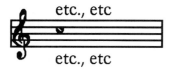

This concept may be extended by focusing on any one of the subdominant or dominant chords used to "extend" the original I chord, and making its root a temporary I. This new temporary I chord root may be preceded by its dominant or a subdominant and dominant "chain."

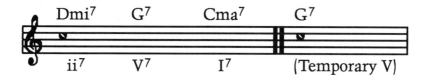

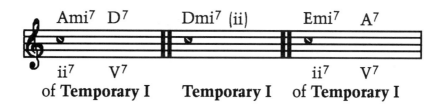

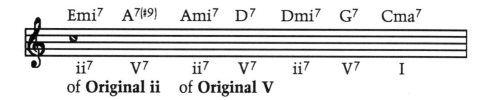

The cycle of fifths also shows the Neapolitan chord as a possibility, and it may be added here for further extension.

Dmi	G	C
ii	V	I

Emi^7	E$^{\flat}$13	Ami^7	A$^{\flat}$7	Dmi^7	D$^{\flat}$7	Cma^7
ii^7	N^7	ii^7	N^7	ii^7	N^7	I^7
of **Original ii**		of **Original V**		of **Original 1**		

PROJECTS

1. Fill in the space with the appropriate chord using the V^7 of the chord following the space.

    E$^{\flat}$ma^7, _____ , Fmi^7, B$^{\flat}$7, Fmi^7, B$^{\flat}$7, E$^{\flat}$ma^7

2. Fill in the spaces with the appropriate ii^7 borrowed from the major key.

    E$^{\flat}$ma^7, _____ , C^7, Fmi^7, B$^{\flat}$7, Fmi^7, B$^{\flat}$7, E$^{\flat}$ma^7, _____ , B$^{\flat}$7

3. Fill in the spaces using the N^7 in replacement of the V^7.

    E$^{\flat}$ma^7, _____ , Fmi^7, B$^{\flat}$7, Fmi^7, B$^{\flat}$7, E$^{\flat}$ma^7

4. Fill in the spaces using borrowed ii^{7}s with regular V^{7}s.

    E$^{\flat}$ma^7, _____ , C^7, Fmi^7, B$^{\flat}$7, Fmi^7, B$^{\flat}$7, E$^{\flat}$ma^7, _____ , B$^{\flat}$7

5. Fill in the spaces using vii instead of V.

    E$^{\flat}$ma^7, _____ , Fmi^7, B$^{\flat}$7, Fmi^7, B$^{\flat}$7, E$^{\flat}$ma^7

6. Fill in the space using VII (or borrowed vii) instead of V.

   E♭ma⁷, _____ , Fmi⁷, B♭⁷, Fmi⁷, B♭⁷, E♭ma⁷

7. Fill in the spaces using ii of vii.

   E♭ma⁷, _____ , E°⁷, Fmi⁷, B♭⁷, Fmi⁷, B♭⁷, E♭ma⁷, _____ , D°⁷

8. Fill in the spaces using borrowed ii of vii.

   E♭ma⁷, _____ , E°⁷, Fmi⁷, B♭⁷, Fmi⁷, B♭⁷, E♭ma⁷, _____ , D°⁷

9. Fill in the spaces using borrowed ii of VII.

   E♭ma⁷, _____ , E♭ma⁷, Fmi⁷, B♭⁷, Fmi⁷, B♭⁷, E♭ma⁷, _____ , D♭ma⁷

Further Substitution

V⁷sus

The V^7 chord may be **suspended** and used in place of the standard V^7 chord. The suspension concept comes from a long practice in sixteenth- and eighteenth-century contrapuntal writing of "suspending" the third of the chord up by a half step before it "resolves" down to the third of the chord. The sound of the suspended V^7 chord has become standard in popular music and is an option for dominant substitutions.

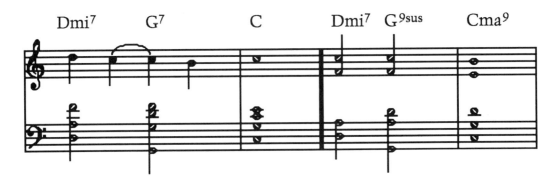

This chord may appear in different notations such as

$$\frac{\text{D mi}}{\text{G}}, \frac{\text{ii}}{\text{V}}, \frac{\text{IV}}{\text{V}}, \frac{\text{F}}{\text{G}}, \text{G}^{\text{sus4}}, \text{G}^{11}, \text{ or } \text{G}^4$$

The suspension may appear in its triad form without the seventh present, as well.

ii of the Neapolitan

As discussed in the preceding chapter on chord substitution, the Neapolitan seventh chord, or N^7, may be used as a substitute for V^7. Through the secondary dominant principle, we may expand the concept to include the **secondary area principle**. The secondary area principle allows for a chain of *secondary subdominant* and *secondary dominant* chords to emphasize a temporary tonic area or chord.

When the harmonic rhythm allows the elongation of a secondary area, both the ii^7/N-V^7/N and the ii^7-V^7 may be used before arriving at the temporary I chord. In other words, both the root of the V^7 and the root of the N^7 may appear as temporary dominant areas before arriving at the temporary I area. This use of the secondary chain of ii-V *implies* both of these dominants, but never actually uses the dominants themselves, before arriving at I.

When both the ii^7-V^7 of the Neapolitan and the diatonic ii^7-V^7 are used, it will appear that an odd tritone substitution has been made. Analysis will show that the V of the Neapolitan and the diatonic ii^7 chord are a tritone away; they should not be seen or analyzed together, but in accordance to their ii-V and secondary ii-V chains.

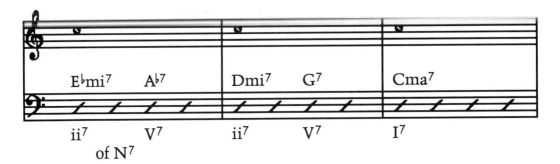

This same technique of the secondary area may be applied to vii° chords when they are used as the dominant. The vii° or the VII chord may act as a temporary V chord and be preceded by its ii chord. This chord will then resume its vii° function and resolve to I in the expected manner.

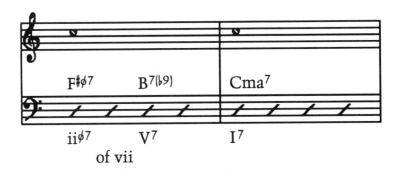

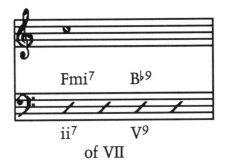

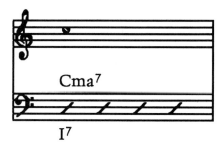

This secondary II-V area concept is satisfying to the degree that the root movement is strong. Some authentic cadences are stronger than others, thus more satisfying. If a secondary II-V area is built on a less satisfying cadential root movement, then the whole chord progression is likely to be less satisfying as well.

Here is a list that indicates dominant to tonic root movement in order of strength.

V-I	Strongest
N-I	Very Strong
VII-I	Good
vii-I	Good
v-I	Weak

Polychords

The stacking of two different chords on top of one another is referred to as a **polychord**. This occurs most frequently in popular music with the dominant chord. In other words, V^7 and the N^7 may be "stacked" either with both chords complete or with one complete chord over the other's root.

$$\frac{G^7}{D^{\flat 7}}, \ \frac{D^{\flat 7}}{G^7}, \ \frac{G^7}{D^\flat}, \ \text{or} \ \frac{D^{\flat 7}}{G}$$

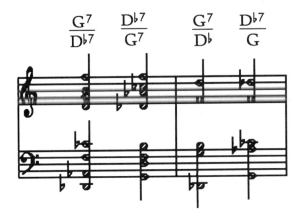

Planing

Another type of chord substitution employs the use of **planing**. When a chord is planed, the actual voicing, and usually the quality of the chord functioning as the temporary I chord, or the arrival chord, is dragged *chromatically* up or down however many half steps the rhythmic pattern dictates. This "consistency" of chord voicing is an aural icon of its own and needs no functional explanation or justification.

This type of chord substitution is used primarily as a voice-leading device. It may function as an alternative means to part-write a nonchord tone in melodic passages, or serve as a "comping" (rhythmic accompaniment) device over a rhythmically static point, adding color, energy, and movement between chord changes.

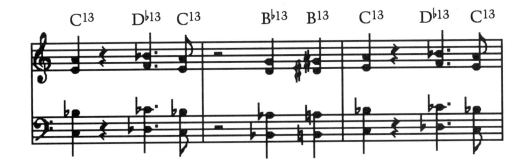

Nonfunctional, Passing Harmony Techniques

Through the concept of planing, many doors open for artificial or nonfunctional chord voicings to be manipulated with regard to passing harmony. Melodic sections can be harmonized using a technique contrived from a constant relationship, which may be either *linearly based* or *vertically based*.

LINEAR RELATIONSHIPS In a **linear-based relationship**, the melody is assigned a **constant** or **variant** set of relationships to its harmonic color. Using the constant-set concept, the melody note might be assigned to be a ♯9 of each chord that harmonizes the melodic segment. This will create a **constant relationship** to the harmony that is not concerned with functional harmony as it relates to the overall tonality.

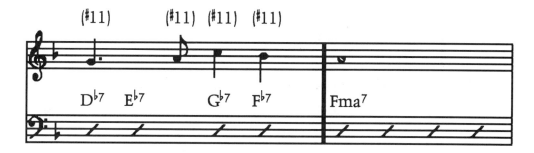

In a **variant set of relationships**, the melodic segment may be assigned a set of numbers that is to reflect the chord extension that the melody represents. The segment is then harmonized using the set of numbers as the constant, creating a structure that is logically and aurally intriguing, but organized outside of functional harmony.

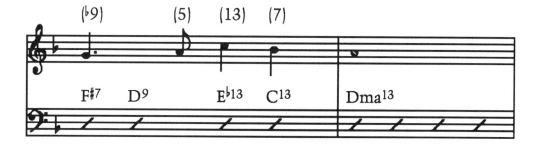

VERTICAL
RELATIONSHIPS

In a **vertical relationship**, the organization of structure ignores the melody, to the extent that the melody is now just a chord member, whether diatonically spelled or enharmonically spelled, and focuses on the chord voicing as its base of aural logic. This concept may also be divided into two categories, the **constant** and **variant structures**.

Polychords may be used to harmonize a melodic segment; thus, a vertical relationship is formed. In a **constant structure**, the vertical polychord construction will remain constant throughout the melodic segment being harmonized. The construction of the polychord can be anything the composer/arranger desires: for example, a triad on top of a bass note, where the bass note is a whole step above the root of the upper triad, the root of the upper triad that is a whole step above the bass note, both upper and lower structures that are half steps apart, a minor third apart, a Perfect fourth apart, etc.

Constant Structure/Bass Whole Step Above

Constant Structure/Bass Whole Step Below

Constant Structure/Polychords Half Step Away, etc.

In a **variant structure**, the polychord relationships will be random, depending on the bass line desired. This creates a "wash" of passing motion that has an abundance of useful tension.

Variant Structure/Bass Below

The linear constant and vertical constant relationships previously described have used a bass motion parallel to the melody curve. When the bass motion is contrary to the melody curve, more tension is created. In other words, the concepts discussed may be used in a manner that places the bass motion in an opposite direction from the melodic motion.

Constant Structure

Variant Structure

Diatonic Inversion of Chords

The most overlooked and rarely associated chord substitution is not really a chord substitution at all. An inversion of chords is used to give movement to the bass line without actually changing chords. If the progression C⁷ to Fma⁷, or V⁷ to I, is used, many performers, arrangers, and producers will place the third of the C⁷ chord, or $\frac{C^7}{E}$, in the spot where a substitution might be placed.

This has the bass moving up by a half step to the I chord, which is similar to vii to I root movement. Here the E, in the bass, is an inversion of the V⁷ chord and not a root of a chord.

PROJECTS

1. Create a V-I motion-chord progression using V⁷sus.

2. Take the chord progression built in project 1 and respell it as $\frac{ii}{V}$.

3. Take the same chord progression and respell it as $\dfrac{IV}{V}$.

4. Take a ii^7-V^7-I chord progression and insert before the diatonic ii^7 chord, the $\dfrac{ii^7}{N}$ - $\dfrac{V^7}{N}$.

   Example: Dmi^7-G^7-Cma^7 becomes $E\flat mi^7$-$A\flat^7$-Dmi^7-G^7-Cma^7.

5. Take the chord progression used in project 4 and transpose it to all twelve keys.

6. Build a chord progression using the secondary ii-V area concept as it would apply to the resolution of vii-I.

   Example: $F^\sharp mi^7$-B^7-Cma^7.

7. Build the same chord progression as it would apply to the resolution of VII-I.

   Example: $E\flat mi^7$-$B\flat^7$-Cma^7.

8. Take the example $\dfrac{D\flat^7}{G}$ and transpose it to all twelve keys.

9. Take the example $\dfrac{F^7}{B}$ and transpose it to all twelve keys.

10. Build a V^7-I chord progression using the first inversion for the V^7 chord.

    Example: $\dfrac{C^7}{E}$ to Fma^7.

11. Transpose the progression built in project 10 to all twelve keys.

12. Reharmonize the given melody in a manner suggested in a linear-constant non-functional approach.

13. Take the melodic segment in project 12 and reharmonize it using a linear-variant nonfunctional approach.

14. Take the melodic segment in project 12 and reharmonize it using a vertical-constant nonfuctional approach.

15. Take the melodic segment in project 12 and reharmonize it using a vertical-variant nonfunctional approach.

16. Take the melodic segment in project 12 and reharmonize it using an approach of your choice, but placing the bass in contrary motion.

12
Pedal Point and Ostinato

Pedal Point

Pedal point is the technique of sustaining one pitch while harmony passes through the pedal. The pedal point may be on the *tonic* or *dominant* pitch and may be in the *bass* or *soprano* or *middle* registers. The pitch may be **inactive**, such as the constant sustaining of the one pitch, or **active**, having a rhythmic pattern or octave duplication.

Inactive/Bass Pedal

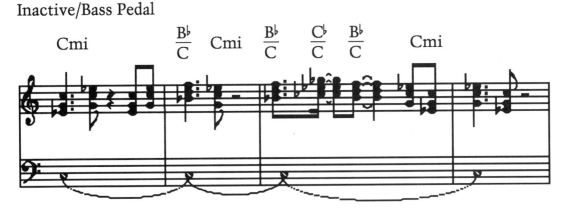

Inactive/Soprano Pedal

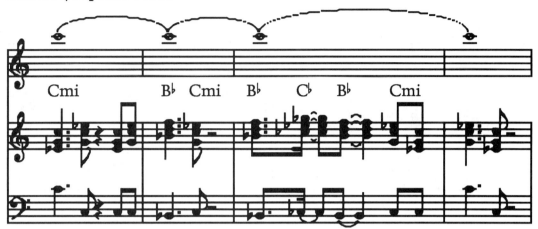

Inactive/Middle Pedal

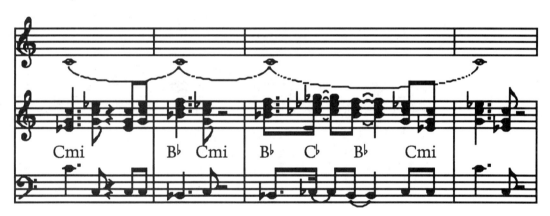

Inactive/Bass Dominant Pedal

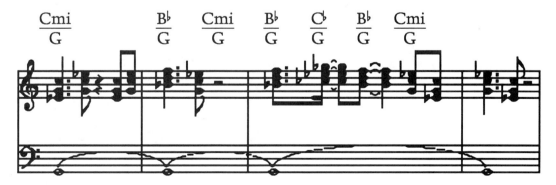

Inactive/Soprano Dominant Pedal

Inactive/Dominant Pedal in Middle Range

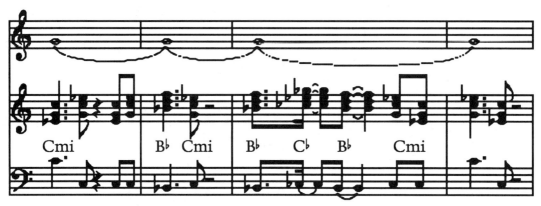

Active/Bass Tonic Pedal

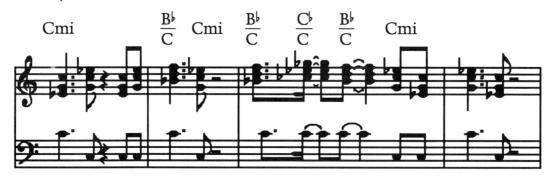

Active/Bass Dominant Pedal

Ostinato

Ostinatos, like pedal points, involve repetitive passage work. Unlike pedal point, an ostinato employs the repetition of a group of notes or a phrase, while a pedal point will use a smaller number of notes. An ostinato acts as a phrase unto itself, repeating constantly in whatever register it is found. Ostinatos, too, may appear in the lower, upper, or middle registers.

The musical and emotional effects of an ostinato are similar to that of a pedal point. They both create harmonic tension. Both techniques derive their notes from the harmony that is employed.

Bass Ostinato

Ostinato in Soprano

Ostinato in Middle Range

Both pedal point and ostinato techniques create a suspension of harmonic motion with regard to aural effect. The overall sense is one of marking time. These techniques are most often seen in the introductions of arrangements, at modulation points, interludes where musical pauses or character changes occur, or during thematic statements or developments.

Pedal point and ostinato may be used together. The pedal point will be seen in the bass voice, while the ostinato will be in the soprano voice or vice versa. It is most convincing when both the pedal and ostinato are on the same pitch function, tonic or dominant.

PROJECTS

1. Use the following progression and create a tonic pedal point in the low, middle, and upper registers: I-vi^7-ii^7-V$^{7(alt.)}$-I

2. Transpose your three examples to the parallel minor key.

3. Using the progression in project 1, create an ostinato and place it in the lower, middle, and upper registers of a major key.

4. Transpose your examples to the parallel minor key.

5. Create a progression of your choice and build both a pedal and ostinato into the passage.

Part Three
Melody

13

Melodic Manipulation

Melodic Construction

The creation of a melody is a gift and a craft. The gift of melodic creation cannot be taught and has its origins in a composer's awareness of things around him/her, his/her past experiences, both musically and nonmusically, and the composer's intuitive capacity. The craft of melodic writing can be taught and is based on analysis of successful melodies, from which theories may be derived.

Melody is one of the most important of the basic elements of music. Melody and rhythm are the basic elements that are complete unto themselves, that have life, and that maneuver their way into the human psyche. It takes only a hum or whistle or even a thought to bring a melody to life. Melodies may exist in thought without being expressed through an instrument. Melodies have the power to stimulate memory, express the deepest and most powerful of feelings, create desire, and bring peace. It is one of the few things known that can bring about so vivid an emotion without being associated with words. When words are added to melody, a marriage is made of two powerful forces, creating the most potent communication art that exists.

For these reasons, the craft of melodic construction is of premier importance. It is unfortunate that this craft is taught so rarely. Most instructive time is spent in training a student in voice-leading tendencies in order to create smooth, effective, efficient part motion. This is of great importance as well, but is subordinate to the creation of a powerful melody in the first place.

Never forget that intuition is the most generous of gifts. When an idea comes to you as a composer, drop everything and write it down; the time needed to fully develop that idea will come, but the idea itself may pass. The idea may be a fragment or a complete phrase or more. Develop the habit of writing the idea down as quickly and as accurately as possible. The pain of a forgotten melodic gem is not soon erased. A person's intuitive capacity will increase in direct proportion to the time invested in listening, analyzing, and playing or singing. Intuition will grow in complexity as time allows for maturity and absorption of stylistic elements. Having given intuition its due, what remains to be developed is craft, and this is what this portion of the book will try to do.

Melody is a constant factor in commercial and popular music. It is the ultimate responsibility of every participant of any ensemble, whether his or her function is that of composer/arranger, horn player, keyboard player, bassist, drummer/percussionist, or even engineer. Everyone is responsible for melodic flow, contour, rhythmic accuracy and flow, intonation and interpretation—whether the part is written and thus in need of interpretation, or improvised and in need of spontaneous stylistic creation.

Basic Elements

There are some basic elements that need to be absorbed and mastered with regard to melodic creation. (Many of these concepts in melodic manipulation may also be applied to the areas of form and rhythm within a piece through the macro-micro concept.) These manipulation principles have been in use for a very long time and may be applied without regard to style.

Repetition

To create length without coming up with brand new material, a phrase, portion of a phrase, or rhythmic idea may be *repeated exactly*. This device doubles the amount of existing material without requiring that an equal amount of new material be written or played. One of the strongest values of this device is that through repetition, the musical idea becomes stronger in the listener's memory. A person's mind needs reinforcement of a certain thing before it can be easily remembered. The brain must have a certain degree of repetition of stimuli before it has the opportunity to recall it quickly. Thus, in melodic repetition, the more hooks, bridges, choruses, etc. that are repeated in whole or in part, the more weight they carry with the listener. This is one of the primary principles behind companies spending such enormous amounts of money on advertisements that include musical signatures to represent their products and then paying to have them broadcast so often. Through the repetitive presentation of their product and music the consumer builds a familiarity and identification with that product and will eventually be more likely to buy that product.

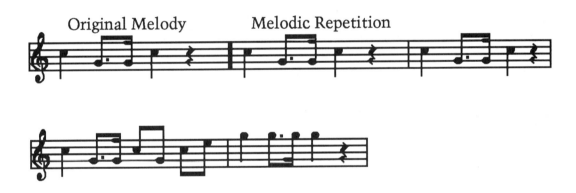

The *blues* has traditionally been one idiom in which the repetition of melodic material, either exactly or in slight variation, is most obvious. **Blues** is most often a twelve-bar form consisting of two contrasting ideas, A and B, each phrase consisting of four bars. The A phrase melody is usually repeated exactly or in slight variation over different harmonic changes to give added emphasis before receiving the musical answer or response to the A phrase, thus completing the musical thought for that cycle of the form. The A phrase repetition adds weight, recognizability, and even tension before resolving or having the thought come to a close.

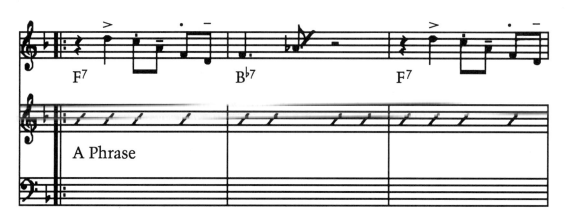

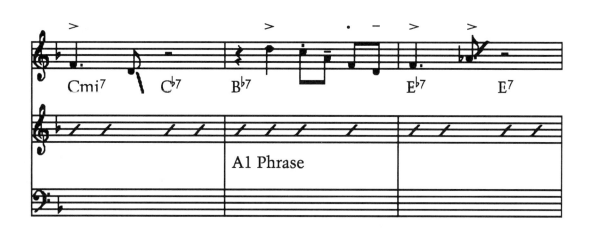

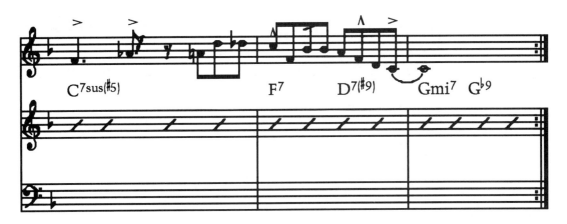

Augmentation and Diminution

Two other skills that are effective in deriving additional melodic material from a single idea include *augmentation* and *diminution*. These are rhythmic devices as they apply to an existing melodic portion.

To apply the **augmentation** device, the original melodic idea is extended rhythmically. The first natural selection is to double the rhythmic value of the original. This may be considered to be **strict augmentation**. Another approach may be considered **random augmentation**, where the rhythmic values of the original are extended, but at points that are new and different, without strict regard to the original values.

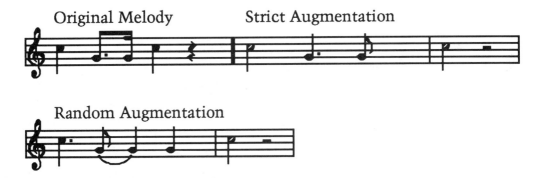

The **diminution** principle is like the augmentation concept except in reverse rhythmically.

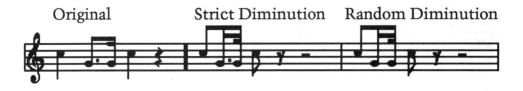

These two principles exist in time and do not affect the pitch relationships at all.

Inversion and Retrograde

Inversion and retrograde apply to the manipulation of notes themselves with regard to another version of melodic material, be it the original melody or some derivative. **Inversion** technique deals with the placement of notes in the opposite direction of another melody, up or down. This reversing of the direction of pitch may be in exact proportion, as is the case in *exact inversion*, or relative proportion, as in *diatonic inversion* and *random inversion*. **Retrograde** is melodic manipulation through the idea of starting at the end of a melodic portion and progressing backwards.

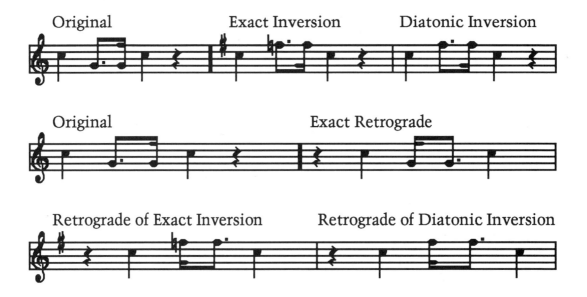

Transposition and Fragmentation

Two other techniques that are effective in creating more interesting melodic material are *transposition* and *fragmentation*. Using the technique of **transposition**, any phrase or phrase portion may be transposed to another pitch level. The transposition may be:

1. *exact*,
2. *diatonic*, or
3. *mixed*,

depending on the complexity and color of your piece.

In an **exact transposition**, the intervalic integrity of the original is maintained. If the original phrase begins with a Perfect fifth skip up, then the exact transposition of the phrase will begin with a Perfect fifth skip up, beginning on the new first note and continuing forward.

In a **diatonic transposition**, the tonality of the piece, or section of the piece, is maintained. The intervals of the original melodic phrase are adjusted chromatically to fit the tonality, modality, or chord spelling when an adjustment is necessary.

Mixed transposition is a combination of both exact and diatonic transposition. The intervals used are either exact in quality from the original or altered chromatically in some manner, or both. The ear and taste of the composer/arranger and the aural needs of the piece at that moment will determine the quality of intervals throughout the transposed segment.

The use of this technique usually occurs when harmonic considerations are not of prime importance. In other words, if your piece, or section of a piece, is being written with just melody or counterpoint as the basis for musical interest, the use of mixed transposition may be useful. If harmony and chord changes are an important factor as well, diatonic transposition technique may include mixed transposition already within it.

Original   Exact Transposition

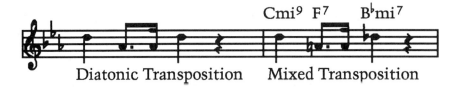

Diatonic Transposition   Mixed Transposition

Fragmentation is, as the name implies, the use of a portion of a phrase or melody. Melodies can be written using fragments of the original and manipulating these fragments to create interest, length, and tension.

Sequences

Melodic **sequences** can be created through the fragmentation of an original melody and following that fragment with a diatonic transposition of that fragment, and still another transposition, either exact, mixed, or diatonic. This creates the melodic sequence before reaching that phrase's climax through new material. The use of sequences is a marvelous technique that has been used for centuries to create interest and it adds to the recognizability of a melody, which is paramount in commercial music. Also, for example, if our original phrase was stated somewhere in the piece, fragments of the original could be used along with its repetition, transposition, inversion, retrograde, etc. to create background figures that could function as horn lines, string pads that have rhythmic interest, background vocals, and so forth. This type of melodic manipulation gives continuity to a composition or arrangement and glues all of the figures together as a unified whole. It creates the impression that all of the figures in the arrangement were made to go there and were not just pulled out of a hat and stuck in the chart because "well, it just felt like *something* had to go there."

Original   Fragment   Sequence

Nonharmonic Tones

Melodies may include scale passages, modal passages, or intervalic sequences, such as a pattern of ascending or descending thirds, fourths, etc. These strongly recognizable patterns build strength and security within the melody. Confidence is also built into melodic structure when a melody contains a substantial portion of notes that are chord members. However, too many chord tones can bring on boredom, and thus the quest is to find the appropriate proportional balance between harmonic and *nonharmonic* tones.

The term **nonharmonic tone** refers to a melodic tone that is not a chord member. It will function as a temporary dissonance within the chord tones. The use of nonharmonic tones can bring rewarding emotional gestures to the music due to the presence of tension within the music created through the interplay of consonance and dissonance. This jousting of consonance and dissonance is the primary source of drama and interest within melodies. These devices may be used regardless of the musical style in which the composer is working. They have been used for many years as techniques of creating interest melodically.

Nonharmonic tones may be generally classified into two categories: those that occur on strong beats and those that occur on weak beats. *Passing tones, anticipations, neighbor tones, changing tones,* and *escape tones* are among those seen on weak beats.

WEAK-BEAT NONHARMONIC TONES

Passing tones are the nonharmonic tones that are most often seen in music. Every melody, either complex or juvenile, is likely to possess many passing tones. When a melody is stepwise in either direction and within that stepwise passage there occur chord tones and nonchord tones, the nonchord tones are said to be "passed through" in order to arrive at the chord tones.

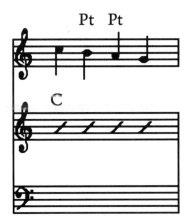

An **anticipation** occurs when a nonchord tone that appears as a dissonance in one harmony is tied, usually over a bar line, to the same note, which becomes a consonance or chord tone within the changed harmony. The chord tone of the second chord arrives before the actual chord does, and thus "anticipates" its arrival through a tie.

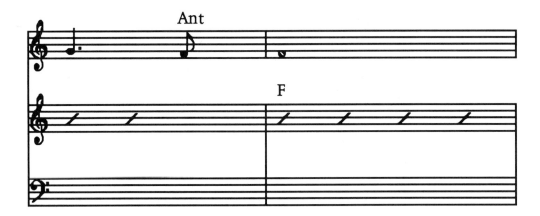

A **neighbor tone** is a nonharmonic tone that leaves a chord tone either up or down by a step before arriving back to the same chord tone, usually on the weak part of a beat. If the motion is from a chord tone to a dissonance a step above and back again to that chord member, the nonharmonic tone is referred to as an **upper-neighbor tone**, whereas the motion from a chord member down to a nonharmonic tone by step and back again is called a **lower-neighbor tone**.

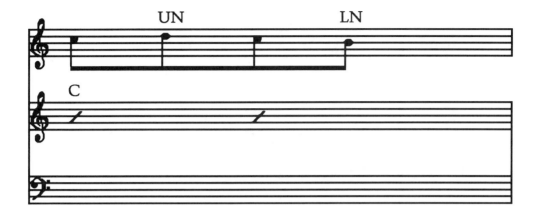

The **changing tone**, also known as the **cambiata**, may be identified as a nonharmonic tone that occurs on the weak beat and that
leaps to another nonharmonic tone before resolving to a chord tone
by step.

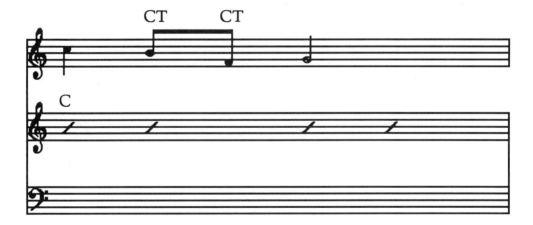

Like the changing tone, the **escape tone** has two names. It is
also known as the **echappee**. These names apply to a nonharmonic
tone that occurs on the weak beat, steps away from a chord tone,
and then leaps to its resolution of a chord tone. The stepping away
from one chord tone will be in the opposite direction of the leap
toward the resolution.

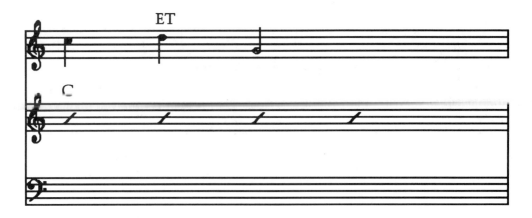

STRONG-BEAT
NONHARMONIC
TONES

The *suspension, appoggiatura,* and *accented passing tone* will occur on the strong beat or beat portion.

The **suspension**, as has been discussed in many sections of the book—primarily in Part II (Harmony), regarding V⁷ˢᵘˢ chords—refers to its distinctive sound quality. This nonharmonic tone sequence begins on the weak beat or weak part of a beat and will be prepared through the tying of a chord tone. This tied note will become a nonharmonic tone within the new chord, on a strong beat or beat portion, at either a fourth interval above the root of the new chord or a ninth interval above the root. Its resolution sequence begins downward by a step either to the third of the new chord, as in the case of the fourth interval, or to the octave, as in the case of the ninth interval. This too will occur on the weak beat or weak part of a beat. These two types of suspensions are referred to, respectively, as a "4-3" suspension and a "9-8" suspension.

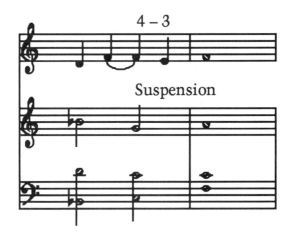

Suspension

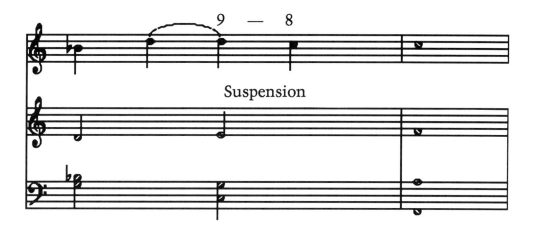

Suspension

Appoggiatura is a term referring to a nonchord tone that occurs on a strong part of a beat, usually the downbeat, and is approached by a leap before resolving to a chord member by step. The leap preceding the nonchord tone may be from either direction, up or down.

App.

This is not to be confused with an **accented passing tone** type of nonharmonic tone. The accented passing tone is a nonchord tone that also occurs on the strong beat before resolving to a chord member, usually on the weak part of a beat, but is approached by a step.

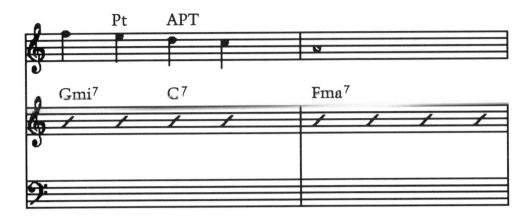

Rhythmic Displacement

Other techniques that are useful in focusing a new melody's character involve attention given to discovering its rhythmic potential. When a raw idca for a new melody is written, it may look like this:

Some questions need to be addressed so that the "first draft" might be refined.

1. *Should the melody start on the downbeat of beat one?*

Rarely is it a good idea to begin any melody on beat one. Doing this tends to lock the rhythmic life of the melody into a box. Usually, it will be best to start somewhere else, anywhere else, than on the downbeat of one. When the melodic rhythm of a phrase begins somewhere else, many rhythmic doors open for a melody. Life is added to the rhythmic flow and a sense of forward motion is created.

Techniques useful in deciding where to begin the phrase are *anticipation* and *delayed attack*.

Anticipation, in its rhythmic meaning, refers to the shifting of the beginning note forward rhythmically, or "anticipating" its entrance. There are several ways to experiment with this in order to determine which is the best for your melody.

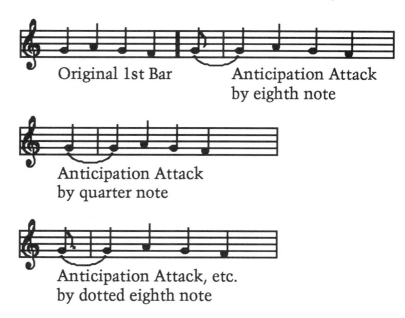

Original 1st Bar   Anticipation Attack
                         by eighth note

Anticipation Attack
by quarter note

Anticipation Attack, etc.
by dotted eighth note

Using a **delayed attack** is the reverse concept of anticipation and may be used effectively as well to add a different color or character.

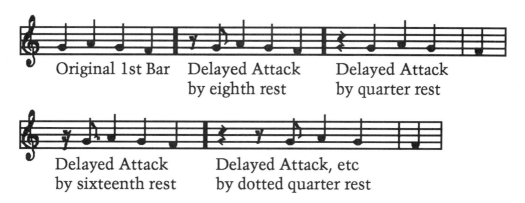

Original 1st Bar   Delayed Attack   Delayed Attack
                    by eighth rest   by quarter rest

Delayed Attack   Delayed Attack, etc
by sixteenth rest   by dotted quarter rest

2. *Is my melody too boring?*

Some spice may be added to the melody by the use of rhythmic *syncopation*. **Syncopation** refers to the displacement of a rhythm from the downbeat to the *preceding* or *following* offbeat. This may be accomplished by using a subdivision of eighth note, sixteenth note, or triplet (sixteenth-note, eighth-note, quarter-note, and half-note triplets).

Syncopation is the rhythmic lifeblood of commercial music and a thorough understanding of the concept and execution of syncopation is a *must* for all performers and writers.

3. *Does my melody have space to breathe?*

Melodies do indeed need space to breathe. Drama and expectation are also created through the use of space within a melody. Learn to incorporate space within your melodies, not too much space, but enough. This can be done in a melody that has too little space by inserting rests. By the same token, take rests out and move on with your rhythmic flow in a melody that has too much space.

Changing Time Signatures

To create melodic development and to check to see if the character of the melody is best served in the manner in which it exists in the first draft, change the time signature and see if it will help the rhythmic flow. Several different meters exist. **Duple meters** are meters that have a pulse that is basically a feeling of two beats per bar with 2/4 and 4/4 time signatures as the most common duple meters. **Triple meters** have a flow of three beats per bar as in 3/4, or its twin 3/8, as well as 6/8, 9/8, and 12/8 as the most common triple meters.

Mixed meter as a device can be useful in creating certain emotional qualities. **Mixed-meter** writing allows for changes in the melodic phrases from one time signature to another.

PROJECTS

RHYTHMIC AND PITCH ALTERATION

Use the following melodic portion as the basis for Projects 1–9.

1. Expand the melodic portion given into a longer melody through the device of repetition.

2. Rhythmically alter the melodic portion given by using the augmentation techniques:
   (a) strict augmentation
   (b) random augmentation

3. Rhythmically alter the melodic portion given by using the diminution techniques:
   (a) strict diminution
   (b) random diminution

4. Alter the pitches of the given melodic example by using the inversion techniques:
   (a) exact inversion
   (b) diatonic inversion
   (c) random inversion

5. Alter the pitches of the given melodic example by using the retrograde techniques:
   (a) exact retrograde
   (b) diatonic retrograde
   (c) random retrograde

6. Alter the pitches of the given melody by using the fragmentation techniques:
   (a) diatonic fragmentation
   (b) exact fragmentation
   (c) mixed fragmentation

7. Alter the pitches of the the given melodic example by using the transposition techniques:
   (a) exact transposition up an interval of a minor third
   (b) diatonic transposition up an interval of a Perfect fourth
   (c) random transposition down an interval of a major third

8. Pick any bar of the melodic example given and create three different sequences of that bar using the selected bar as the first portion of each sequence.

9. Take all of the exercises that you have written so far in projects 1-8 and apply one other technique to each exercise, creating a new version of your melodic material.

NONHARMONIC TONES

Use the following melodic portion as the basis for Projects 10–13.

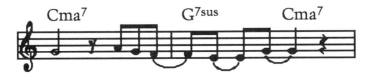

10. Use the melody provided and insert the following strong-beat nonharmonic tones as desired:
    (a) passing tones

(b) anticipations
(c) upper neighbors
(d) lower neighbors
(e) changing tones
(f) escape tones

11. Use the melody provided and insert the following weak-beat nonharmonic tones as desired:
    (a) 4-3 suspensions
    (b) 9-8 suspensions
    (c) appoggiaturas
    (d) accented passing tones

12. Use the melody given as a point of departure and alter it by employing several of the techniques in both projects 10 and 11 in order to create a new melody.

13. Take this newly created melody and employ several of the techniques in projects 1–8.

RHYTHMIC DISPLACEMENT

Use the following melodic portion as the basis for Projects 14–17.

14. Using the melodic example given, change the first bar by using the anticipated-attack technique and the delayed-attack technique.

15. Alter the rhythm of the given example through the use of the syncopation technique. Use both syncopation prior to the beat and syncopation after the beat.

16. Add rests to the syncopated version of the melody you wrote in project 15.

17. Take the melodic example you created in project 16 and change the time signature of that example at least twice.

14

Melodic Contour

Strong melodies contain certain observable tendencies. Of course, there are no specific rules that pertain to how a perfect melody may be created; yet many techniques can be documented that may be of help to the composer when inspiration is "out to lunch."

Melodic Rhythm

A melody cannot exist solely through pitches sounding in certain orders. These pitches have to be synchronized to a rhythmic flow. This rhythmic flow breathes life into the pitches through the element of time. Therefore, there can be no separation made between rhythm and pitch order. Rhythm can exist by itself without pitch, yet melody must be a marriage of these two elements.

Before a strong melody can be composed, you have to create a logical and flowing rhythmic pattern or sequence on which to place beautifully organized pitches. One way of creating a logical and pleasing rhythmic flow is to select a standard rhythmic pattern on which to anchor and to build your melody. There are many rhythmic patterns from which to choose as a starting point and they exist in all cultures and reflect the purpose that they serve within a culture. For example, a hymnlike rhythm can suggest a stately, majestic, serious, inspiring, or calming character. It may find itself laying out into logical, short and well-defined phrases or sections. A lullaby type of rhythm will more than likely be in a triple meter, slowly flowing in a repetitive pattern that lulls one into quiet relaxation through a cyclic sectionalized form. This is the point of a lullaby. A waltz, on the other hand, will be in a triple meter with a moderately quick tempo that has an accent on the downbeat of one. Beat three may also be accented, creating a push over the bar line into beat one. Psychological qualities associated with waltzes may inspire youthful nostalgia, a sense of celebration, love remembered, etc. As you can see, each rhythmic pattern can help inspire an emotional backdrop on which to compose an appropriate melody.

There are rhythmic patterns found literally everywhere in every culture across the globe and in every age of mankind, both past and present. They are also being created all the time. What type of rhythmic flow would suggest a busy, important computerized office or industry? One such type of rhythmic pattern may consist of straight eighth or sixteenth notes, depending on the degree of activity required, and it may have several subpatterns of cross-rhythms within it. These cross-rhythms may be laid out in logical units, each making sense in a cyclic pattern. When these cross-rhythms are played against the basic eighth-note or sixteenth-note pulse, they serve as a reflection of individually efficient tasks being accomplished within an industry.

These psychological associations are being established, for example, by composers of music for industrial films and feature films, and for advertisements for companies that want to establish images of important high-tech activity and innovation. This music, once repeated to a large audience via the media, can create a new psychological association for the public with regard to a rhythmic pattern.

Some sample patterns may include: a waltz, a hymn, a lullaby, a samba, a bossa nova, funk, swing, swing shuffle, black gospel, white southern gospel, marches, ballads, polkas, heavy-metal rock, rockabilly, boat songs, drinking songs, Dixieland jazz, dirges, work songs, blues, etc.

A sample mental list may look something like this:

Waltz – triple meter, downbeat accent, maybe one and three, nonsyncopated.

Jazz Waltz – triple meter with the same characteristics as a waltz, but with added syncopation.

March – straight eighth-note feel in duple meter with an accent on one and three.

Samba – quick Latin feeling in duple meter, based on straight eighth notes, but with a cross-rhythm accent on the downbeat of one and the upbeat of two, possibly realized over a bass pulse pattern of one, the upbeat of two into the downbeat of three, and the upbeat of four into the next one's downbeat.

Bossa Nova – slower Latin feel built on straight eighth notes in duple meter with a primary cross-rhythmic accent on the downbeat of one, the upbeat of two, and the downbeat of four, all repeated.

The list is endless and beyond the scope of this book. Yet, a sensitive composer must be constantly on the lookout for just these rhythmic associations. To the composer, there is always a mental reference file ready to be updated with regard to rhythmic implications.

Composing a Motive or Hook

The most recognizable and memorable part of melody is the **main motive** or **hook**. The hook is the musical microcosm that weaves its way into the human psyche and, through reinforcement, remains there. The hook of a song is what advertisers want floating in your head, what songwriters want tugging at your heartstrings, and what television producers use to get your attention. It is the single most powerful bit of information that music can deliver.

Examples of musical hooks are easy to provide. Try to remember the hook to "Mary Had a Little Lamb," to the McDonald's commercial "You Deserve a Break Today," to the Beatles tune "I Wanna Hold Your Hand," to Michael Jackson's "Beat It," to the title song from "The Andy Griffith Show," to the hymn "Amazing Grace," to Pontiac's "We Build Excitement" advertising campaign, to the theme from the "Tonight Show" starring Johnny Carson, to the main theme of the first movement of Beethoven's Fifth Symphony, etc., etc., etc.

Those first recognizable fragments of the tunes listed are the "**hooks**," and they are aptly named, because you can readily bring them to mind even though you may not have listened to some of these tunes for quite a while. They come to mind because they are well-crafted in their composition, they are well-produced, and they were played for you regularly.

Melodic Shape

A well-crafted melody will possess a contour or shape that will outline and define its inherent points of tension or drama. This shape or contour will fluctuate between different registers—high, medium, and low—through a worked-out plan that builds to a climax or capping-off point. In other words, a good melody will not simply begin at a certain point, constantly climb to a higher and higher register, and then just stop at the highest spot of the instrument's or voice's range. Remember: "What goes up, must come down."

Melodic contour, like most elements in music, is based on a series of contrasts, high vs. low, slow vs. fast, busy vs. calm, etc. These contrasts create interest and tension over time, and they pose, for the musical element involved, a problem or struggle that must be worked out to a successful conclusion. When this tension and release factor is accomplished well, not only has a problem been solved, but the listener has started at a certain point, has been taken somewhere, and has either returned again to that point renewed or has ended up in a new place of interest, having been on a journey.

This movement of melody can possess, to a greater or lesser degree, drama and action, or calmness and serenity, depending on the amount of movement, high to low, and whether or not the motion is acquired linearly or accomplished through leaps and skips within the melody. This drama will be planned and worked out by the composer according to the needs of the musical prescription. Drama is action, both in the degree of pitch and in the degree of rhythmic activity. Serenity is calmness and well-ordered movement with regard to the same elements.

Tension and Release (Leaps and Skips)

Melodic motion can be by a step in either direction. This linear type of motion provides an even and calming quality to the melody. Skips may be used either from chord member to chord member or from chord member to nonchord member. Melodic skips among chord members give the opportunity for relief from just stepwise motion, while still maintaining a degree of calmness. More tension can be created when there are skips from chord member to nonchord member. This creates a dissonant tension between melody note and chord spelling.

Wide leaps of more than a Perfect fourth can add to the tension and dramatic elements within a melody. Leaps among chord members are more dramatic than skips, while leaps from chord members to nonchord members are still more dramatic.

When skips and leaps are employed, there is also a psychological need, eventually, to *fill in the gap with the missing notes*. In other words, if you leap in one direction, sooner or later, the missing notes, or the ones that were leaped over, need to sound. This effect is another idea that is useful to composers. The longer the missing notes within a gap created by a skip or leap are delayed in being heard, the greater the tension. This also implies that when a change in direction is made within a melody by skip or leap, upward or downward, some motion needs to occur to counterbalance that movement in the opposite direction. If you go up, you need to come back down at some point.

There is a psychological need to hear all the pitches within a scale or mode. This desire to hear the entire scale can be used to the advantage of a composer through more tension and release concepts. Tension can be created by delaying the sounding of one or more pitches within a scale until these pitches can be best used to relieve the building tension at the climax point within a culminating phrase.

Phrase Structure

Most melodic ideas (pitches) and their corresponding melodic rhythms will fall into another tension-and-release category. This category has to do with the offsetting of contrasting ideas. Usually, there are two contrasting ideas, enough to provide a basic amount of developmental material, but there may be more. This desire to have contrasting elements is a microconcept that may be employed on either a micro- or macro-scale.

A phrase in popular music is usually eight bars in length. This is enough time to establish a musical sentence. A musical sentence or phrase will possess two contrasting ideas, "A" and "B." Usually, the "A" statement will take four bars to introduce a question, while the "B" statement will also be four bars in length and will serve as the response or answer to the introductory "A" section.

This initial A-B sequence sets in motion a dialogue and is a microcosm of how musical ideas work.

This introduction of the first A-B dialogue serves as the "A" phrase. What will follow depends on the composer's wishes, the musical prescription, and the listener response that is desired. Somewhere there may be a "B" phrase that will function as a response to the "A" phrase and these two musical sentences are enough, once again, to create a useful contrast. There may be more than two musical sentences, each possessing different rhythmic motives and ideas that contrast with each other. There could be a "C" phrase or "D" phrase. The layout of the phrases and the order in which they occur is a matter of form, which is phrasing on a macro-scale. This will be discussed further in a separate chapter.

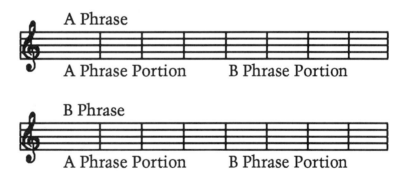

Composing a Melody

Melodies often come out of nowhere while the composer is driving or walking or eating or sleeping. Usually, they come when the mind is at rest or is occupied in some mundane task. However, in the case of most composers in radio, television, and advertising, composing is a fast and furious craft. In either case, skill, taste, quality, and experience are the hallmarks of a great composer.

Sometimes, therefore, things have to be manufactured. This is the crunch time for most composers, *"the deadline."*

Melodies can be crafted by themselves without harmonic considerations or can be composed after a chord progression has been established. Sometimes these will come together. If the melody is composed first, the form and harmonic rhythm and chord choices will follow afterward. If the chord progression is created first, it will possess a harmonic rhythm that may inspire a melodic idea. In either case, a lot of manipulation exists in both of these areas. Rarely does a whole song fling itself on the score page complete and perfect in the first draft. Not many of us have the innate talent of a Mozart.

Melodic, harmonic, and formal considerations have to do with choices made through instinct, curiosity, experience, plagiarism, experimentation, etc. There is a great deal of, "What would it sound like if I did this?" in composition. Only when deadlines are tight does the inexperienced composer rely on past successes and formulas; yet, the more you master formulas and copy successful patterns composed by others, the more your ideas will come fresh and new, already packaged in a workable format. One learns how to do something by emulating the work of those who can already do it.

PROJECTS

1. Try to remember twenty-five songs. If you cannot remember twenty-five, go to some sheet music or collection in book form, or go to your record collection and find twenty-five songs in contrasting styles. Analyze what rhythmic pattern or style is being used in each. Give each tune a name with regards to rhythmic feel.
   Example: The theme from "The Andy Griffith Show"—medium swing, heavy back beat on two and four, "swing" or 12/8 style eighth-note pattern.

2. Pick some rhythmic pattern from one of your twenty-five analyzed tunes and use its rhythmic feel as inspiration for the composition of a new hook. Sing the rhythm in your head for a while until ideas begin to form. Once your ideas begin to come, try to write a strongly recognizable rhythmic motive of no more than two bars. It may be only two beats in length; the duration will vary. Once you have a hook in mind, check to see if it is still interesting after you have repeated the hook, back to back,

four times. Once you are satisfied that the rhythmic idea is very strong, find melody notes that will fit on top of that rhythm. Try all types of combinations—steps, skips, a skip with a stepwise resolution, etc.

3. Take some of the ideas on melody manipulation from Chapter 13 and apply some of these concepts.

4. Take the hook that you have composed in Project 2; it should be no longer than two bars. Treat it as if it were the "A" statement of a phrase. Compose a counter-statement, or response, or "B" statement in bars three and four.

5. Either repeat the "A" and "B" statement in the next four bars or transpose them, but keep the rhythm the same, or compose new material from bar five onward. This will provide you with an eight-bar phrase.

6. In the same manner, compose a "B" phrase consisting of two four-bar "A" and "B" statements. Each statement will have a two-bar "A" and "B" format. You will now have two contrasting phrases.

15
Melodies from Scales and Modes

Melodies can be created from the theoretical relationships found in harmony and from the scales or modes that correspond to those harmonies. These relationships may be used as launch points for the creative urge.

Modes

Modes are basic units of pitch organization that can be employed to stir the creative impulse. Each mode has a corresponding harmonic implication. To begin acquiring skill in modal manipulation, the student must first master modal spelling. There are relationships that are useful in speeding the spelling process.

Each mode may be associated with a major scale through the table at the top of page 127. The intervalic relationships associated with modes will appear automatically when the mode is related to the major scale in this way.

THE IONIAN MODE   If a major scale were to be played on the note "C," then the **C ionian mode** would appear because the ionian mode has become

Mode-to-Major-Scale Relationships

Ionian Mode	= **1st** major-scale degree
Dorian mode	= **2nd** major-scale degree
Phrygian mode	= **3rd** major-scale degree
Lydian mode	= **4th** major-scale degree
Mixolydian mode	= **5th** major-scale degree
Aeolian mode	= **6th** major-scale degree
Locrian mode	= **7th** major-scale degree

the modern major scale. In this manner, an ionian mode may be constructed on any pitch.

C Ionian Mode

THE DORIAN MODE In the remaining modes, dorian through locrian, the mode will possess two names. Much like intervals, these names have *generic* and *specific* meanings. ***The generic name will be the name of the mode being spelled***, and thus its intervalic construction. ***The specific name refers to the pitch on which the mode begins.***

In the table of Mode-to-Major-Scale Relationships, dorian is equal to the second major-scale degree. Therefore, if the note "D" is the second scale degree of the C major scale, the mode D dorian may be spelled by writing the C major scale, and its corresponding key signature, starting on the note "D" and ending on "D." When the C major scale is written from "D" to "D," the intervalic relationships of the dorian mode will magically appear.

D Dorian Mode

THE PHRYGIAN MODE The remaining modes may be spelled in the same manner as the dorian. "E" is equal to the third major-scale degree. Therefore, in which major scale is the note "E" the third degree? To spell E phrygian, the C major scale would be spelled, starting and ending on "E."

E Phrygian Mode

THE LYDIAN MODE   The lydian mode is equal to the fourth major-scale degree. If you wanted to spell F lydian, in which major scale is the note "F" the fourth-scale degree? Clearly, the C major spelled from the note "F" to "F" is the F lydian mode.

F Lydian Mode

THE MIXOLYDIAN MODE   The mixolydian mode is equal to the fifth major-scale degree. If you wanted to spell the G mixolydian mode, in which major scale is the note "G" the fifth scale degree? Obviously, the C major scale spelled from "G" to "G" is the G mixolydian mode.

G Mixolydian Mode

THE AEOLIAN MODE   The aeolian mode is equal to the sixth major-scale degree. If you wanted to spell the A aeolian mode, in which major scale is the note "A" the sixth scale degree? Here, the C major scale spelled from "A" to "A" is the A aeolian mode.

A Aeolian Mode

THE LOCRIAN MODE The locrian mode is equal to the seventh major-scale degree. If you wanted to spell the B locrian mode, in which major scale is the note "B" the seventh scale degree? Evidently, the C major scale spelled from "B" to "B" is the B locrian mode.

B Locrian Mode

Harmony and Its Corresponding Modes

Certain chords may have melodic parallels derived from the modes. For example, *any minor 7 chord, or a chord possessing a minor triad and a minor seventh, will have the dorian mode as its corresponding mode.* The extensions of the minor seventh chord, the ninth, eleventh, and thirteenth, when spelled out linearly will form the dorian mode.

Fmi⁷   F Dorian

Any dominant 7 chord, or a major triad with a minor seventh, will have the mixolydian mode or the lydian ♭7 mode as its corresponding mode(s). The choice of which mode to use will be determined through the desire to write or play "*inside*" diatonically or "*outside*" the tonality. The mixolydian mode serves the dominant 7 chord's tonal role as relating diatonically to a tonic chord, while the lydian ♭7 mode alteration serves the chord as its own dominant entity and provides for the ♯11 extension. The extensions of the dominant seven chord—the ninth, eleventh, and thirteenth—when spelled out linearly will form the lydian flat 7 mode.

D⁷   D Mixolydian

Any **major seventh chord**, or a chord possessing a major triad and a major seventh, will have as its corresponding mode(s) the ionian mode and lydian mode. The ionian mode will serve in the diatonic capacity, whereas the lydian mode will mirror its extended capacity.

Other Scales

Other scales and modes may be used in conjunction with chords. These serve as an introduction to improvisation as well as to melodic composition. The **harmonic minor scale** or an **ascending melodic minor scale** will work over a minor chord with a major seventh.

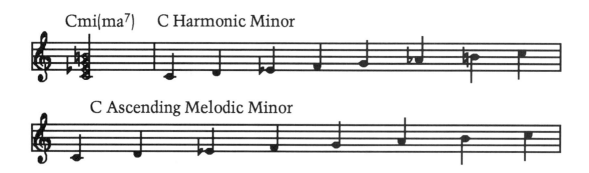

The **natural minor scale** or the **descending melodic minor scale**—they are one and the same—will work over a minor seventh chord.

The **blues scale**, which is the minor pentatonic scale with an added pitch, will work over a dominant 7, ♯9 chord.

The **minor pentatonic scale** will work over any minor seventh chord.

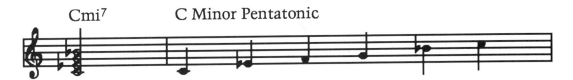

The **major pentatonic scale** will work over any $\frac{6}{9}$ chord.

The **diminished half-whole scale** will work over any dominant 7, ♯9 chord.

The **diminished whole-half scale** will work over any diminished 7 chord.

The **whole-tone scale** will work over any dominant seventh chord with a sharp eleventh or sharp fifth extension.

The **ionian mode** will work over any major triad or major seventh chord.

The **phrygian mode** will work over any minor seventh chord.

The **aeolian mode** will work over any minor seventh chord.

The **locrian mode** will work over any half-diminished seventh chord.

Modal Alterations

In common practice, improvisers have created mutations of standard modes in order to provide more accurately a scale that will quickly facilitate any chord's alterations. These mutations have acquired names of their own. There are many thorough manuals on this subject. A few of these modal mutations will be listed here.

The **lydian diminished scale** is based on the lydian mode, but has an alteration of a lowered third modal degree. This scale works well against any fully-diminished seventh chord.

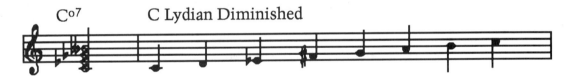

The **locrian ♯2 scale** is based on the locrian mode, but alters the second scale degree up by a half step. This scale works well against any half-diminished seventh chord.

The **super locrian scale** is also based on the locrian mode, but uses a lowered fourth scale degree. This scale works well over any dominant seventh chord with a flatted fifth and flatted ninth alteration.

The **Hindu scale** is basically a natural minor scale with a raised-third scale degree. This scale works well over any dominant seventh chord with a raised-fifth alteration.

PROJECTS

1. Write an ionian, dorian, phrygian, lydian, mixolydian, aeolian, and locrian mode on every pitch.

2. Write a corresponding chord for each of the modes that you have written.

Part Four
Form

16

Blues

Blues evolved as a means of expression by slaves in the Mississippi River area. The blues is a personal means of telling stories and relating emotions such as fear, anger, joy, sorrow, etc. It is now a standard form that comes from two separate styles, *rural blues* and *urban blues.*

Rural Blues

Rural blues is historically played and sung by one person playing one instrument, which may be among the following: guitar, piano, harmonica, or banjo. This type of blues rendering is a style of playing and singing that is orally passed down from generation to generation. It only takes one person to execute, and this style bends to the ability and desire of the performer.

Traditionally, blues has twelve bars of chord material that are repeated exactly to form a harmonic drone or bed. This chordal repetition allows the focus to shift from the rather monotonous chord motion to the words of the singer or the improvisation of the instrumental soloist.

In rural blues, the performers are people who wish to express emotions or stories through an oral medium. These people are generally not musically skilled to any great degree and mostly find pleasure and release through their participation in the blues. This allows for many inconsistencies in the rural bluesman's performance. The form of the blues can vary from ten to thirteen bars or more from verse to verse. This type of inconsistency can only happen and still remain musically and emotionally satisfying when performed by one person.

Urban Blues

Urban blues developed as people traveled up the Mississippi River to more populated areas: Memphis, St. Louis, and Chicago. In these cities there already existed a strong European musical tradition and the audiences open to blues music were more discerning listeners. Also, these towns gave more opportunity for interrelationships among musicians than did the plantations and fields, where the blues performer was likely to be isolated from any musical growth or experimentation. A big development in the differences between rural and urban blues was the availability to the performer of diverse instruments to choose from in the city. The rural-blues performer now had the opportunity to listen extensively to and learn to play instruments not available to him in the country. These changes brought about a shift from the solo rural-blues performer to a group of players performing on acoustic basses, pianos, saxophones, trumpets, trombones, as well as harmonicas and guitars, etc.

With the addition of personnel to the ensemble came a necessity for consistency in form. This necessity brought about the standard twelve-bar blues form.

Harmony

The chord progression of blues is subject to change from player to player as are all chord progressions in standard jazz forms. Jazz is based on the art of improvisation and this concept reaches into the arena of chord progressions as well. These changes can be as simple or complex as desired by the performer; however, there is a base from which to begin or a model to use as a blues progression in its simplest format.

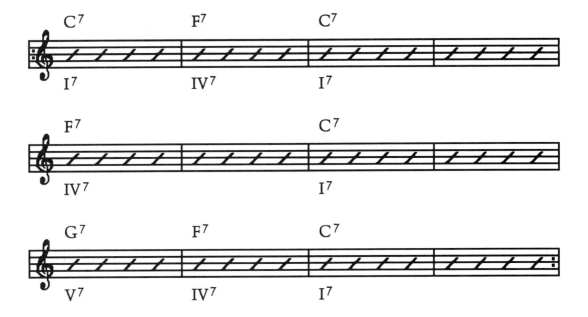

All chord substitution techniques discussed previously can apply to these sets of chord changes. It is a good idea to use several different sets of changes, progressing from the simple to the complex, to accompany a singer or soloist. As the soloist creates more intensity during the course of his or her solo, the substitute changes can give a support base for that intensity as well as provide a bed of creative inspiration.

Melody

The *call and response* concept is a basic element in the blues melodic structure. This concept allows a dialogue between the singer or soloist and the audience or band whereby the performer can make a statement or ask a question, receive a response from the audience or other band member, ask or state it again, and then finish the statement or answer the question in a last phrase. This statement or question would fit into a four-bar phrase (bars 1–4), have that phrase repeated over a different chord change for added emphasis (bars 5–8), and then answer the question or complete the statement in the last four-bar phrase (bars 9–12).

Melodic material for the blues is based on the harmonic material of the *blues scale* discussed in Chapter 15. The blues scale is derived from a mix of African melodic tradition trying to adapt to European harmonic tradition. This mix of cultural backgrounds has formed a distinctly American tradition that is immediately associated aurally with the blues.

The phrase structure and melodic rhythm should remain very verbal to be the most aurally satisfying. Blues is primarily an oral art and its aesthetic quality will stay with that oral reference whether the blues being performed is sung or played instrumentally.

PROJECTS

1. Create your own blues piece using the blues chord progression within the chapter.

2. Create lyrics for your·music by formulating a storyline and synthesize your storyline into the *call and response* format, as illustrated under the *Melody* section of this chapter. This will facilitate the use of several verses, but you should edit these to get the smallest number of verses necessary to complete the idea of the piece.

17
The Popular Song

The popular song is the staple of the commercial-music industry in that its history in this country reaches back to the 1800s. During the course of that history, the success of the popular song has catapulted the music industry into one of the largest money-producing facets of the entertainment industry. The popular song has also weaved its way into the fiber of popular culture. Each generation, regardless of era and musical style of the time, has had its own heroes, superstar performers, and influential composer/arrangers and producers who created the sounds that encapsulated each era for posterity. These songs crystallized the emotions, mores, fads, and attitudes of a generation and can still bring back the essence of the time. People who participate in popular-music culture tend to mark their own personal histories by certain songs that were popular at the time of major events in their lives.

Songs That Last

A successful popular song has at its core a strong and memorable melody, poignant and timely lyrics, and a clear functional form for the tune. These are the lasting factors that, when well-crafted, can lead to not only a "hit," but possibly a "standard" as well. What seems to change most often from era to era and fad to fad is the rhythmic content, the attitude and approach of the rhythm section, and the orchestration techniques. An appropriate balance of each of these factors helps to create the structure for a lasting and memorable song.

The "standards" of popular-music literature have a lasting quality that is brought about by strong compositional craftsmanship. These standards can be just as musically effective when placed in arrangements that may show little resemblance to the original production, yet because of the strength and craftsmanship of the music, the song not only works within the confines of its new setting, but, in fact, it thrives. It is when too much attention and production value are placed on the rhythmic or orchestration aspects of the tune without appropriate regard for the melody, lyrics, and form that a song becomes "locked in," and therefore stymied, from growth or a life outside of its original production. This is not to say that songs with these types of emphasis cannot be hits. Indeed, many times these tunes have strong commercial appeal and may even reflect some aspect of current trends to the degree that these may be perfect examples of the "musical times." Yet, rarely are these songs able to escape the original discs that give them life, and eventually they pass into musical nostalgia.

Labeling System

Melodies fall into phrases, and with phrases there are implied chord changes that accompany those melodies. The phrases that are exactly alike or are very similar in melodic and harmonic content are then related and therefore possess the same structural letter name. If the similarity is not exact and the differences between sections are only superficial, then the sections bearing the similarity may possess the same letter name and have subsections designated by a number sequence. In other words, one section may be labeled as "A" while a similar, but not exact, repetition of that section may be labeled as "A^1," then "A^2," etc.

The first contrasting phrase, after the "A" section, that has new melodic and harmonic material will be labeled "B" or the next letter in sequence, while any similar subsections of this letter will possess a numerical name as well, "B^1," "B^2," etc. (Any lettered phrase section should be considered only with regard to that particular song. All "A's" are not the same from tune to tune with regard to the numbers of bars that are included in the section, amounts of chord changes used, melodic contour, or any other compositional factor.) This system gives an easily recognizable formula for labeling similar and contrasting phrases. Having been acquainted with the labeling system most commonly used in formal analysis, it will be easier to understand the compositional process.

A-A-A Form

Some songs are a complete repetition of the "A" section with no contrasting "B" section to give variety. Any blues tune will be considered to be an A-A-A form. This type of form is commonly employed in storytelling songs.

The "A" section involved in an A-A-A form usually will consist of eight bars or one standard phrase. However, this is not a hard-and-fast rule. Blues tunes, as discussed in a separate chapter, are usually twelve bars in length and have a corresponding subsection within the twelve bars.

A-A¹-B-A Form

The A-A¹-B-A song form may be the best known and it has a long heritage. Here the hook of the song is found in the "A" phrase and that phrase has the most repetitions in order to reinforce the hook within the listener's mind. Each phrase will usually be eight bars in length, and the "B" phrase serves as a release from the "A" phrase.

This type of song form stems from stage forms and from early movie forms that were stage-influenced, in which transition was needed to get from the dialogue within the show to the full-fledged song. This transition was called the **verse** and has its heritage in the operatic tradition of the recitative. The verse functioned as a setting up of the musical situation lyrically and eased the audience into the music portion without having to jump into the body of the song from the cold silence of dialogue. As the audience had time to warm up to the music through the verse, it was ready for the *chorus*, where the real musical weight and hook of the tune resided. What was called the **chorus** of the show tune was often this A-A¹-B-A song form. This is why the hook of the tune occurs in the "A" sections so frequently. The relief section, or the "B" phrase, was called the **bridge** because it provided contrasting material to the "A" phrase and it bridged the gap back into the "A" phrase. So, the components of the original show-tune format were the verse and the chorus.

Hybrids of the 32-Bar Song Form

With the tradition of the verse-chorus format and the establishment of the 32-bar chorus length within that format, composers began to use the 32-bar format by itself when radio became widespread, since it was the real meat of the tune and did not need to have an association with the plot of the script. With just the meat of the song to present over the new media, variations of this 32-bar cycle were inevitable.

These variations were structured for the new media format and included introductory material before the body of the tune arrived, but to a far lesser degree than the stage format. The introduction now only needed to be four to eight bars in length, enough just to set up the song. There may be several different verses or new words for every repetition of the song's 32-bar form in order to present a complete idea lyrically. Within those repetitions of the form, arrangers maintained and heightened listener interest through the insertion of modulations, orchestration changes, chord substitutions, or other production devices. To bring the song to a successful conclusion, some type of ending was created that would affect the length of the tune's 32-bar form within the last repetition.

These compositional changes, inspired by the needs of the new medium of radio and its capacity to make hits and stars, along with these star's live concert presentations of those radio hits, helped usher in a new age of songwriting and production.

A-B-A-B   The A-B-A-B form was developed. This consisted of an eight-bar "A" phrase and a contrasting eight-bar "B" phrase and their repetition. The second "A" and "B" phrases may have some slight differences melodically or harmonically in the second 16-bar sequence. Each of the four phrases were usually eight bars in length providing a total of 32 bars for the song.

A-B-A-C   The A-B-A-C form is another variation of the 32-bar popular song. It has an "A" phrase with a contrasting "B" phrase, a repetition of the "A" phrase, or variation of it, and some new concluding material or "C" phrase. Here each phrase will also usually contain eight bars, for a total of 32 bars within the tune.

A-B-C-D   The A-B-C-D form is an outgrowth of the A-B-A-C form. It usually contains four eight-bar phrases, each possessing new melodic material, for a total of 32 bars. This type of song form is rarer than the others simply because it requires more attention from the listener. There are fewer opportunities to nail home a hook through its repetition, which is the primary function of a popular song in the three minutes of standard-media airtime.

A-A-B   Of course, there are still variations from the main forms just listed and experimentation goes on with every composer of music. An illustration of one type of experimentation that was found to be successful is the A-A-B form. Here, there are two contrasting musical ideas, an "A" phrase and a "B" phrase, and each has eight bars within the phrase structure, as in the A-A-B-A form. However, in the A-A-B-A form, when the tune's form is repeated or cycled, there are three "A" phrases that will appear back to back. The variation of the A-A-B-A form was to have two "A" phrases repeating as the tune's form is recycled from bottom to top, not three. When one of the standard "A" phrases is removed, there is only a phrase structure of A-A-B remaining, with 24 bars of actual music.

Song Forms in Contemporary Production

Today's songwriting uses a different format and labeling hierarchy. For example: in the past, the form of the tune would be completely repeated and lyrics would be written to accommodate the entire song's form. Production and arrangement decisions fitted into that form to create color and momentum. Today, the actual form of a tune may only be stated one time and the remaining part of a song, consisting of fragments of that tune's form, inserted according to the wishes of the producer, songwriter, recording executives, etc. The "A" phrase will usually still be eight bars and will contain verse material. The "B" phrases may vary in length and will contain the chorus and hook material. The *"C"* phrase will vary in length and will be used to offset the sounds of the "A" and "B" phrases. *Form, then, is looked at per song, in its entire length, and not in regard to "song form," as in some basic pattern of compositional architecture.*

For example: the standard A-A-B-A form, if repeated, would look like A-A-B-A/A-A-B-A/A-A-B-A, while today the songwriter might use the form A-A/B/A/B/C/B-B, or A-A/B-B/A^1/B^1-B^1-B^1, or B/A-A^1/B-B^1/A/B-B, or A-A^1-A^2/B/C/B-B^1, etc. The number of "A's" and "B's" indicate how many times that phrase is repeated.

PROJECTS

1. Write one song in each of the forms discussed in this chapter.

2. Create a new form not listed here, and see if it will work well.

18

Jingles and Advertising

Music in Advertising

With the exception of publicly financed stations, radio and television have to advertise to survive. It is the lifeblood of the industry. Without local or national companies buying commercial spots on television and radio, there would be little money to produce TV shows, pay the D.J.'s, and buy equipment. These entertainment industries exist to advertise products and services to as large an audience as possible.

This airtime, whether in the form of radio or television commercials, is usually divided into small segments of sixty seconds, thirty seconds, fifteen seconds, and sometimes five seconds. These units of time are the most affordable for the advertiser and the least likely to alienate the audience. Sixty- and thirty-second "spots" have traditionally been the standard advertising time units; however, there have been and always will be changes made within the industry from time to time.

The prices for these units of airtime range according to the audience size. There will be a huge difference in price between the cost of a sixty-second spot for "Bob's Pizza Emporium" on a local cable channel during reruns of "The Addams Family" at 2:00 a.m., and the cost of that same spot for McDonald's at halftime of the

147

Super Bowl. Yet, both Bob's and McDonald's are looking for the same result from their advertising investment—more business!

The image of the company and its product will be determined by the quality of the advertisement that is aired. Many factors are involved in producing an advertisement of even thirty seconds in length. The perceived quality of that spot is determined by the imagination and skill of the people creating the spot and the resources available from the company that it will represent.

It is a competitive and rewarding market in which to work. The production time is usually very small and the people involved have to work at a tremendous pace. Those at the top of this business are incredibly skilled and imaginative individuals who excel in stressful situations.

Music for these advertisements is written and produced to fulfill the specific needs of each commercial. This means that there are no standard formats for accomplishing the goals of a successful advertisement. However, some trends can be presented to illustrate examples of successful advertisements.

Jingles

The term **jingle** refers to a small tuneful song with lyrics that represent a company, product, or service. As stated earlier, music has the power to stimulate memory when it is repeated often enough. Advertisers use the power of melody to place their product or service inside the minds and memories of the people who will potentially use that product or service. A jingle will obviously have a hook, a strong one, and it will be placed as many times as possible within the advertisement.

A jingle is used within the industry typically for "hard selling." This means that its function is to acquaint the public with the product or service as plainly and boldly as possible; to state who makes it, whom it is for, and what it does. In the case of "Bob's Pizza Emporium," Bob is looking to sell pizza and to get the pizza-buying public in his area to come exclusively to his emporium instead of "Joe's Roadhouse Italian Deli" across town. In essence, the airtime Bob purchases from the local country-music radio station and the jingle that he buys will serve as an aural billboard, in lieu of an insert in the local newspaper. He will air his advertisement as often as he can afford to in order to plant the hook of his jingle into the pizza-buying public's ear while they drive their cars.

A typical form for "hard sell" jingles is the **donut**. A sixty-second donut may either start with a short introduction or begin right on top of the hook. Here, the hook will be set to the lyrics of Bob's logo or catch phrase, like "Bob's Pizza Emporium—good food and good fun." Following the hook there may be some verse material used to expound on the quality of the food and service at Bob's, before returning to the hook once more. After the second hook, there will be some music-bed material with no lyrics in order to allow Bob to add a voice-over announcing this week's special attraction or price. This will be followed by the hook one more time before closing.

This sixty-second format will be written with the idea that Bob can have his jingle edited into a thirty-second, fifteen-second, or three- to five-second spot without rerecording the entire jingle. This is how the graph of Bob's donut jingle form will look.

INTRODUCTION *(optional)* + 1st HOOK + VERSE +
2nd HOOK + BED + 3rd HOOK = 60 seconds.

The amount of time from the beginning of the spot through the second hook should be 28 to 29 seconds. This will be the thirty-second spot. The length of the hook itself should be three to five seconds. This is another "edit." For one price, Bob gets a sixty-second jingle with voice-over space, a thirty-second jingle with no voice-over, and a product "ID" of three to five seconds. Bob can use any of these edits according to his advertising budget and marketing plan. It works equally well for radio or television when video or film footage is combined with the audio track. This donut type of jingle structure is and has been the staple of local advertisers for years. Sixty seconds, thirty seconds, fifteen seconds, and five seconds are generic quantities of airtime. In actuality, the time of music will be one to two seconds shorter in order to accommodate "ring time" at the end of the last note in the spot and a slight delay of the audio track at the beginning of the spot. This delay insures that the entire audio track will be heard without any cutting off of the first attack when the film or video is begun at the station. The total amount of time is the larger amount, but the audio track has these smaller adjusted time frames within it.

Larger companies also use jingles but the marketing concept may change more frequently. For example, McDonald's comes up with a new jingle concept almost every year. That jingle will highlight this year's slogan or image slant. They may also use a jingle to promote the addition of a new product. The slogan and consequently the hook of the jingle will change every season; e.g., *McDonald's, Food Folks and Fun, You Deserve a Break Today*, or *At McDonald's, We Do It All for You.*

In a large national campaign, this year's slogan or ad idea will be recorded in a jingle form, but there will be many versions of that jingle. In other words, the main jingle song will be composed for this year's campaign, but the same melody and hook ideas will be rearranged and recorded for many different consumer markets. In this way the same hook and idea will be set to the music style most communicable to that group of consumers.

A company that advertises on a large aggressive scale could have hundreds of edits of the same jingle idea in different styles and lengths. In this manner the company is assured of a positive image in all of the demographic arenas.

Some advertisers change their music regularly, but stay with the same short musical ID or logo, weaving it into every advertisement they produce.

The Image Statement

The national advertising market is comprised primarily of companies that have made it their strategy to advertise regularly and thoroughly in order to keep their company's name in public view. These companies use a different approach in their ad campaigns.

Car manufacturers need not hard-sell their product all the time. There may be several marketing concepts designed to sell the car. Pontiac is not faced with the same advertising problem as "Bob's Pizza Emporium." Bob has to inform the public of *who, what, when* and *where*. Pontiac primarily needs to advertise the *why* of the product. Why should the consumer buy a Pontiac instead of the other domestics or imports? Pontiac is faced with the problem of imaging, or creating an effective image for each car model it manufactures. Many times the image sells more than the product.

Music can be written to create many different images for products. It can help illustrate the sensation of driving and owning a luxury car, the pleasantness of having your living room smell of flowers instead of a wet dog, the honest down-home feeling you get from eating one particular kind of sausage in the morning, or the feeling of being a good wholesome "Norman Rockwellian" mother when you buy and serve a brand of oatmeal.

The donut is not as appropriate a tool for this situation. The music for imaging advertisements is mostly *film scoring*, with the addition of the company's ID hook weaved somewhere within the spot, usually at the end. Advertisers who buy national spots often are accustomed to having their musical ID or logo presented to people. If a consumer watches a certain television show regularly, he or she is going to see the product, hear the name, and hear the logo ID. Without the need to have a hook repeating in an advertisement as often as possible, the composer can concentrate on setting the musical image for the product.

Film Scoring

The term **film scoring** refers to music written to accompany visuals—usually film or video-footage. It is a generic term that applies to a style of composition appropriate to a feature or industrial film, television show, or advertisement. The music need not carry the entire load of the message; there is a combined effort of two elements: the *concept* of the music together with its corresponding image and the *technique* involved in writing, recording, and editing the music. (The technique of film scoring is a broad and fascinating subject that is beyond the scope of this text; there are several very good manuals, such as the Karlin/Wright book, *On the Track*, that discuss this topic in great detail. The compositional concept of the music is more in line with this book's mission.)

Writing for film necessitates a conceptual understanding of when and where to place music in the footage, and then how to accomplish musically the imaging task required.

CONCEPTS IN
FILM SCORING

In any piece of film or video the composer will work closely with some type of overall producer. The title of that producer may vary according to the size and scope of the production house or agency. The composer's job is to provide music that will fit the dramatic, comic, or imaging concepts determined by the producer in charge of the entire project. In most cases several of these ideas and intents are already presented to the composer through storyboards, as in the case of advertisements, or through sample film footage, as in the case of television shows or film projects. Timing break-downs, indicating the length and placement of the music, will be provided by the music editor of the project.

The storyboard and the film footage, or **work print**, will have indications of any specific hits that need to be highlighted within the musical piece. These hits serve as specific points of action or dramatic interest within the overall production. A composer will first take these hit points and their corresponding timings within the film or storyboard, and begin to brainstorm as to how he/she will musically affect them. These hit points provide the first landmarks or structural skeleton for the music. Secondly, the composer will view the work print, or imagine how the visuals in the storyboard will look, and attempt to get certain impressions about the piece that will help guide his or her decisions musically. These impressions may be in the form of rhythm, speed of action, the degree of urgency or melancholy, hardness or softness of camera cuts and angles, underlying psychological state of the characters involved, if any, etc.

From these impressions the composer will then be faced with the task of interpreting and translating the impressions into music that will fit the needs of the picture. This translation process will work itself out in the answering of questions like: What is the tempo of this scene? What rhythmic idea will best serve to drive or underscore the picture? What harmonic and melodic language best fits this mood? What will the shape of the piece be in terms of motion and climaxes?

Once these kinds of questions have been answered, the musical ideas that these questions have spawned can be merged with the structural elements of the hit points in order to begin writing. Many composers take the hit points, find where they lie in the score, based on the tempo chosen, and write backwards from the hits to the beginning. For others, the music comes with rhythmic, melodic, harmonic, orchestrational, and structural aspects flowing all at once. This type of immediate intuition comes with experience and confidence.

Every composer that views the same picture or storyboard will have different ways of scoring the music. It is this individual insight and dramatic intuition combined with masterful skill and craftsmanship that make film scoring such a challenging and personally rewarding endeavor.

Examples of well-crafted imaging campaigns include commercials for McDonald's, Diet Coke commercials, Honda, and Infinity, as well as public-relations campaigns for special-interest groups, such as Amnesty International.

PROJECTS

1. Videotape popular and award-winning television shows regularly. Make sure to get varying time slots so that the range of advertising will include national, regional, and local advertisements. Analyze each advertisement in terms of its compositional content; whether it's a hard-sell jingle or a scored-imaging ad; what is the form of the jingle; in what ways does the jingle vary from similar hard-sell jingles; what is the quality of production and recording; what are the unique technical elements of the piece. Comment on other synthesizer or orchestration tricks, mixing aspects, vocal-performance quality, etc., etc., etc. Only through this type of analysis can any ideas and intuitions be acquired.

19

TV and Film

The Role of Music

Television shows, feature films, documentary films, and industrial films possess much of the same musical content. Music provides continuity and mood for the picture and helps to provide insights into a character's state of mind or identity, as Wagner's music did in the composer's middle- and late-period operas. It can help smooth out transitions between scenes or establish an accurate period setting along with the costumes, makeup, and architecture. It also can help attract a viewing audience, boost box-office sales, and provide peripheral income to the production through record sales, airplay royalties, sheet-music sales, and the like with the inclusion of a hit song within the picture or show. Altogether, music is of critical importance to a production dramatically, structurally, and economically.

Television shows and films usually will have these structural points in common: an opening-title piece, a closing-credit piece, and an underscore at the beginning, ending, or within scenes that will mirror and accent the pictorial content. These production elements are uniform for films, miniseries, hour dramas, half-hour dramas, sitcoms, documentaries, some soap operas, and even cartoons. These kinds of shows need to have the music scored freshly every episode in order to meet the scenes' dramatic requirements, except for the main title and closing credits, which can remain the same from episode to episode.

Certain types of TV shows will have some, but not all, of these elements. For example, game shows, talk shows, news broadcasts, sports programming, informational broadcasts, and some soap operas need not be concerned with underscore in a scene, but need only a main title, closing credits, and ins and outs to and from a commercial. These types of shows can have their music "in the can" already, with different versions of the ins and outs to use as needed, and can edit them into the show almost instantaneously. This kind of show doesn't need a composer to score it every week.

A single composer may be required to provide the main title, the closing credits, and "the score"—the part that is used to accent the drama within scenes for a film or television show—or these elements may be divided among several different composers.

In television, the decision regarding the music will be made by the show's producer or executive producer during the pilot process. A single composer may provide all of the musical requirements for that pilot show, or else one composer may provide the opening title and credit music, which are sometimes chosen through the auditioning of several different themes, while another composer will provide the scoring for the dramatic elements. Also, a composer may provide all of the show's musical elements for the pilot episode, may have the good fortune to have the show picked up and run for a season or more, then may become too busy to continue providing the weekly score for the show, and have that element given over to another composer while the show is still running. In this case the established music for the opening title and closing credits will still belong to the original composer.

For a feature film, one composer may write all of the film's music or it may be divided among several composers: one for the scoring of the scenes, one for the opening title and closing credits, and one for the feature song or songs, if needed, within the body of the movie.

Scoring Drama

The basic difference between dramas and other types of films and TV shows centers around the inclusion of dramatic scoring for scenes. Some shows need it and some don't. This is the element that requires the most creativity and sensitivity from a composer with regard to the production's psychological and dramatic demands.

The creative and compositional aspects and approaches involved in the scoring of drama can vary according to the intuition, insight, and skill of each composer. The choice of who will provide that element for the production, then, is a difficult and weighty decision. The producer will base it on a composer's experience, track record, ability to work with others, ability to work creatively and on time, and the production's budget. There are two sensitive skills that need to be acquired when a composer begins to score drama.

The first problem is how to score for dialogue. The craft of scoring for dialogue presents many opportunities for decision making. Decisions are made as to *whether or not the scene needs music at all*. A poignant scene can be easily ruined by an insensitive composer's intrusion. Dialogue alone is often dramatic enough. If the producer, music editor, and composer all decide that music should be used, then the decision as to how much and what type of music has to be made. How much music can refer to the music's "busyness," its weight orchestrationally, the speed and range of the melody, as well as the supporting rhythms.

All of these musical elements—the nature of the rhythmic speed and activity with regard to both melody and harmony, the range and scope of the melody, the thickness or lightness of the orchestration, etc.—can range from less dramatic, simple, and sweet to very dramatic, grandiose, and powerful, according to how much of each element is used. Also, the reverse is true. The music and its inclusive categories of elements can help add special psychological effects to the picture by going in the opposite direction. Satire can be accomplished when a grand sweeping heroic type of orchestral music is used to portray a bumbling and idiotic marshall riding horseback into the sunset. These types of opposites can be useful in portraying psychosis, simple-mindedness, innocence, pensiveness, or poignancy. A sensitive composer needs to know just what effect each musical element contributes to the overall muse.

Main Titles/Closing Credits

The accompanying music for the main title of a film or TV show can fall into two categories: a popular-song type of format in which the main title could function as a separate entity apart from the picture or a format resembling more of an orchestral overture, in which the thematic material functions as a driving force into the body of the picture and is structured so that it cannot exist apart from the entity it serves. Within these opposite poles there is also a vast amount of variance. What type of music to use for the main title is an artistic decision that will be made according to the overall effect and intent of the picture.

The music for the closing credits is similar to the opening title's music in that it functions as the summing up of the picture or show. It is responsible for leaving the audience with its last impression of the picture. Here, the music may take the form of a duplication of the main title's music, a similar popular-song-form production, or a completely new piece of music structured to sum up the psychological impact and motion of the picture. Silence can also lend strong support to the running of credits. This, too, is an artistic decision.

In television, the main title will last approximately one minute for half-hour dramas and sitcoms, while for hour dramas and miniseries it could be longer. There is no specific formula and this decision is up to the producer. Some networks may also have preferred guidelines for all of their shows. This time frame also holds true for the closing credits. In film, each case will be different, according to the needs of the production.

Feature Songs

Some films choose to include one or more feature songs within the body of the film. This is done to heighten the dramatic elements of the picture as well as to bring in revenue. The song can either be subtly woven into the fabric of the picture or can be obviously placed in a music-video type of approach. Again, both extremes mark opposite poles, indicating a great amount of space for variation in the middle.

Movies can spawn not only "hits," but "standards" as well for artists, songwriters, and their publishers. These movies, if they are hits, will be seen by millions of people and consequently will serve as a huge vehicle for the presentation of music. A great percentage of this audience might hear this song only in the theater and not turn on a radio or buy a CD or cassette. Each time they hear the song they will associate the song's emotional content with the dramatic elements of the picture, giving the song an even greater psychological impact than could be had by the same song's presentation on radio alone. This is the very reason music-videos exist, to place music and a visual aid together for greater impact. A movie has a lot more time to build motion within the plot and set up the music's impact, however. This is why it is still the most powerful way of exposing a new song; thus, the competition for acquiring one of these coveted spots within a film is extremely fierce.

Pictures that have contained these types of hits or standards include: *The Summer of '42, Footloose, The Wizard of Oz, Dirty Dancing, Casablanca,* and most of the Disney movies.

PROJECTS

1. Videotape popular and award-winning television shows regularly. Analyze the music within the show with regard to: when and where is music placed; how the composer scores dialogue and action; what musical elements are employed compositionally that help the overall effect succeed; what is the length and format of the main title and closing credits; are the main title and closing credits the same or different; if they are different, in what way and why; and how effective is the composer in serving the needs of the picture.

2. Watch movies of all types and eras regularly. Analyze the movies in the same manner as was described in Project 1.

3. Begin to put together a list of your favorite composers in this medium. Think specifically about why you have chosen favorites. What merits their inclusion in your list?

4. Read other instructional manuals regarding the mechanics of film scoring, such as those listed in the bibliography.

5. Isolate scenes from a TV show or movie that you wish to score yourself. Turn off the sound on your TV set or video monitor and begin to go through as much of the process of creating your original score as you can. Play it back against the silent picture with as much synchronization as possible, and see how well you've accomplished your objective.

Part Five
Orchestration

20 Acoustic Orchestration

Acquiring skill in orchestration is vital for every composer or arranger. The ability to orchestrate accurately, imaginatively, and under budget restrictions requires an experienced and knowledgeable artisan; yet, the ability to think well and create in orchestral terms begins early through the development of an individual's curiosity.

The ability to orchestrate beyond the realm of the normal brings light and color to any music. Color is brought to music through the individual character and timbre of the instrument itself as well as the musician who performs on it.

Families of Instruments

Instruments can be divided into families or groups. Each family will possess similar qualities due to the nature in which the instruments create sound. In the **acoustic instruments**, or instruments that require no electricity to produce their sounds, there are seven basic groups: **voices**, **strings**, **brass**, **percussion**, **woodwinds**, **keyboard instruments**, and **fretted instruments**. Within each family there are subgroups of individual instruments that possess varying pitch ranges from soprano to bass.

There will be notes that overlap between various instruments within a family. For example: most of the woodwind family can play the note "middle C"; yet, when each does, each will possess a different sound quality and character. Therefore, the choice of orchestration is determined by the character and quality of the instrument assigned to play any passage and its corresponding psychological color and effect. Understanding these nuances is the responsibility and domain of the orchestrator. When the composition is well-crafted, its orchestration is chosen thoughtfully and imaginatively, and the performance given on the instrument(s) by the artist(s) is passionate and of high quality, then there will be a moment of musical magic.

As there is an abundance of excellent manuals on the subject of orchestration, such as those listed in the bibliography, and because the technical aspects of it are beyond the scope of this book, the intent of this chapter is to help establish a healthy curiosity for the subject—to introduce the craft and illustrate the wide variety of choices available to the composer or arranger of commercial music.

The Percussion Family

The **percussion family** is comprised of a wide variety of instruments that produce their sounds through many different means. This family of instruments may be struck with a stick, as in the case of a drum, struck with any type of mallet, as in the case of timpani, jingled, bowed, shaken, blown, etc. The percussion family of instruments is the most varied and diverse and it possesses the widest range of sound timbres and means of creating the sound.

DRUMS   The **drum subgroup** of the percussion family encompasses many instruments that have varied ethnic and cultural origins. Drums are of ancient lineage and they have individual characters. If the drum is handmade, no two drums will be exactly alike in timbre and nuance. They are also thought by some cultures to possess some of the spirit of the drum maker within them. Today, most drums are mass-produced to exacting specifications by commercial drum manufacturers and can be placed in standard categories.

Here is a partial list of standard drums commonly used in commercial music: **snare drums,** varying sizes of **tom-toms,** varying sizes of **bass drums** (also called **kick drums**), **timbales**, **bongos**, **congas**, **Roto toms**, and **timpani** (of various sizes). These are instruments that are constructed using a stretched membrane across a shell of varying dimension and composition. They are played by striking the membrane or shell with either a stick, of various sizes, shapes, and densities, a hand, brush, or mallet. The membrane used may be of substances ranging from animal skin to some forms of plastic or other fiber. These membranes may possess some type of additional sound reinforcement or coloration affecting their timbres or they may be designed to expand and contract, thereby creating the ability to alter their pitch.

WOODEN PERCUSSION INSTRUMENTS   Other percussion instruments are made of wood alone. They differ in their timbres by shape, density, and type of wood. They may also have some other friction component made from materials other than wood. These instruments may be played by striking with a stick, striking against each other, rattling, shaking, etc.

Here is a partial list of *wooden percussion instruments*: **cabasas**, **maracas**, **vibra slaps**, **fish**, **castanets**, **claves**, **woodblocks**, **guiros**, and **temple blocks**.

METALLIC PERCUSSION INSTRUMENTS   Another subgroup of the percussion family is that of metal instruments. These instruments vary in size and shape and method of play, but have as their primary resonating timbres the sound of metal.

Here is a partial list of **metal percussion instruments: wind chimes, double wind chimes, Chinese bell trees, handmade key sets, triangles, cowbells** (of various sizes), **go-go bells**, and **sleigh bells**.

MELODIC PERCUSSION INSTRUMENTS   Another subgroup of the percussion family is one whose instruments possess several pitches and can be used melodically. These instruments may be of wooden or metallic construction, of tubular or block construction, and may be played with mallets of varying sizes, shapes, and consistencies.

Here is a partial list of these **melodic percussion instruments: chimes** (or **tubular bells**), **vibraphones**, **marimbas**, **xylophones**, **bells** (or **Glockenspeils**), **celestes**, and **timpani**.

CYMBALS   **Cymbals** have an ancient heritage as well and were of primary importance in the East. In conjunction with drums, they have become the most commonly used percussion timbres. Cymbals are made from metal alloys of varying composition, and are played by striking against each other, by striking with a stick or mallet of metal or wood, or by other friction-generating procedures, such as bowing or stroking with a brush or coin.

The sound and timbre of cymbals vary according to the metallic alloy used in creating the cymbal, the shape and diameter of the cymbal, and the method of playing the cymbal. Standard commercial cymbal manufacturers place cymbals in the following categories: **concert cymbals, suspended cymbals, ride cymbals, crash cymbals, high-hat cymbals, splash cymbals,** and **gongs.**

OTHER PERCUSSION INSTRUMENTS

Another subgroup of percussion instruments includes those that make sounds not corresponding to any of the other categories. In this category, almost anything that makes a noise, if its timbre is found to be pleasing and musically useful, could be employed as a percussion instrument. A partial list of some normally nonmusical sounds that have been used in compositions as percussion instruments will include: an **anvil**, a **train whistle**, a **canon**, a **lawn mower**, a **car horn**, a **whip,** and an **air horn.**

FUNCTION OF PERCUSSION INSTRUMENTS

Percussion instruments serve two basic functions with regard to their musical and orchestrational purpose:

(a) to perpetuate rhythmic flow and
(b) to highlight and punctuate, or draw attention to, a particular musical passage.

In the (a) function, that of perpetuating a rhythmic flow, the percussion family can be a primary source of interest, contributing to the drive and fabric of the music, through its unique ability to create time. No other family of instruments can provide the basic musical element of rhythmic activity through time, without being tied to pitch, as well as the percussion family. *When percussion is used as a coequal partner to other melodic instruments it can contribute rhythmic activity and development on a contrapuntal level to melodic instruments.*

In the (b) function, that of highlighting and punctuating a particular passage, *the percussion family serves as a coloration for the activity of other instrument groups.* It can provide a wide variety of color and emphasis to draw attention to an important passage. In this capacity, the percussion usage is supportive and noncontrapuntal.

The String Family

The **string family** is a group of instruments made of wood. These instruments have four strings of varying dimensions stretched across the wooden frame. This family is subdivided into individual string instruments that produce a pitch range from lowest to highest. The pitch range of each instrument is determined by the size of the wooden frame and the length and dimension of its strings. The string family corresponds to the acoustic properties of the laws of physics; thus, the longer the string, the lower the pitch.

The **violin** is the *soprano instrument* of the string family. It has a range of more than four octaves beginning on the G below "middle C." The violin is written in concert pitch and in the treble clef.

The **viola** is the *alto instrument* of the string family and possesses a range of more than three octaves beginning on the C below "middle C." The viola is written in concert pitch, but in the alto clef.

The **cello** is the *tenor instrument* of the string family and it has a range of more than four octaves beginning on the C an octave below the viola. The cello is written in concert pitch in the bass clef.

The **double bass** is the *bass instrument* of the string family and has a range of over two octaves beginning on the E below the low C of the cello. The double bass is written one octave higher than it sounds in the bass clef.

These instruments are primarily bowed, but may be plucked or snapped by the fingers as well. A variety of effects is possible through the use of **mutes, trills, tremolos, harmonics, multiple stops,** or more than one note sounding at once, and different **bowing techniques** including: *deteche, loure, staccato, saltando, saltato, spiccato, jete, ricochet, col legno, pizzacato, sul ponticello, martellato,* and *sul tasto*.

The function of the string family is primarily to carry the melody or provide chordal and contrapuntal support to other instruments or voices.

The Brass Family

The **brass family** is comprised of a group of instruments that create their sound by the buzzing of the lips into a mouthpiece. This buzzing is then channeled through metal tubing and leaves the horn through a bell which serves as amplification for the tone. Different pitches are produced by the degree of lip tension and the length of tubing in the instrument; the longer the tube, the lower the pitch.

The **trumpet** is the *soprano instrument* of the brass family and has a range that is dependent on the ability of the player. Professional players will be able to play at least two and a half octaves some players over three—beginning on the F below "middle C" concert pitch. The B♭ trumpet is written a whole step above the concert or sounding pitch.

There are various types of trumpets. The standard trumpet is the **B♭ trumpet**, which was just described. Trumpets can be found in **C, D,** and **E♭** as well. These are mostly orchestral instruments that are used for their different timbres and can be useful in playing certain orchestral literature. The **cornet** and the **flugelhorn** are two different types of trumpetlike instruments. The cornet is used primarily in wind-ensemble and marching-band literature, while the flugelhorn, a softer, more mellow-sounding instrument, is used frequently in jazz and commercial music. Both of these instruments have roughly the same range as the trumpet, except in the uppermost register, and are written in the same manner as the trumpet. The **piccolo trumpet** is pitched in B♭, as is the B♭ trumpet, and plays one octave higher than the B♭ trumpet. It is written a minor seventh below the concert pitch.

The **French horn** is the *alto instrument* of the family and possesses a range of over two and a half octaves beginning on the F at the bottom of the bass clef, concert pitch, depending on the player. The French horn is written up a Perfect fifth from the sounding or concert pitch.

The **trombone** is the *tenor instrument* of the family and has a range of over two and a half octaves beginning on the E, one ledger line below the bass-clef, concert pitch, depending on the player. The trombone is written in concert pitch.

The **tuba** is the *bass instrument* of the brass family and has a range of almost three octaves beginning on the D two octaves below the D in the bass-clef staff, concert pitch. The tuba is written in concert pitch. There are several different types of tubas, but the most commonly used is the BB♭ tuba.

All brass instruments can alter their sounds through the use of *mutes*. **Mutes** are inserted into or over the bell of the instrument, thereby altering or coloring the sound as it exits the instrument. Several different types of mutes exist including: the *straight mute,* the *cup mute*, the *Harmon mute*, the *whisper mute*, the *wah-wah mute*, the *plunger*, and the *bucket mute*. Some of these mutes may not apply to all of the brass instruments.

The Woodwind Family

The **woodwind family** is comprised of subgroups of instruments that produce their sounds in varying ways. The manner of sound production ranges from blowing into or across a hole in the instrument's mouthpiece, creating a whistling-like sound; blowing into a mouthpiece that contains a single reed of cane attached to the flat, stable surface of the mouthpiece; or blowing through two cane reeds loosely attached to each other, forming a mouthpiece. The characteristic timbre of each woodwind instrument will be shaped by its means of sound production.

THE FLUTE FAMILY

The **flute family**, or subgroup, is a group of instruments that use the blowing of air across a hole in the instrument as the method of tone production. The flute family boasts its own distinct timbres that have a wide range from the most soprano, downward.

The **piccolo** is the most *soprano instrument* of the family, with a range of almost three octaves beginning on the D in the staff of the treble clef. The piccolo is written one octave down from where it sounds.

The **flute**, or **C flute**, is the *standard instrument* of the family and it possesses a range of over three octaves beginning on middle C. It is a nontransposing instrument and it is written where it sounds.

The **alto flute**, or **G flute**, is longer and, therefore, *lower in pitch* than the other two flute family members. It has a range of three octaves and is written a Perfect fourth above where it sounds. This is a hauntingly beautiful instrument that is not very powerful. Therefore, it has found favor more in the recording studios, where its volume and timbre can be boosted and properly mixed with the whole, than in the live medium.

THE SINGLE REEDS

The **single reeds** classify the two subgroups of instruments that produce their sounds through the vibration of one cane reed against the flat surface of the mouthpiece on which it is attached. The degree of vibration, equating into pitch, is therefore controlled by the mouth tension of the player and the amount and speed of the air column that is forced between the reed and the mouthpiece.

The Clarinets

The **clarinet subgroup** of instruments uses this type of tone production in conjunction with a wooden instrument of varying length. The length of the instrument, with the appropriate-size reed and mouthpiece, determines its range.

The family member with the *highest range* is the **E♭ clarinet**. It has a range of over three octaves beginning on the G below the treble clef. It is written a minor third below the sounding concert pitch; this is the most soprano instrument of the family.

The **B♭ clarinet** is the *standard instrument* of the family. It possesses a range of over three and a half octaves beginning on the D within the bass-clef staff, and is written a whole step above the concert, or sounding, pitch, in the treble clef. The B♭ clarinet could be considered the *alto instrument* of, and is one of the most used instruments of, the family.

The **B♭ bass clarinet** has a range of over three octaves beginning an octave below the B♭ clarinet. It, too, is written in the treble clef and, therefore, is written a major ninth above the sounding pitch. This instrument could be considered the *tenor instrument* within the family.

The **E♭ contrabass clarinet**, or the **contralto clarinet**, is the lowest practical instrument of the family. It has a range of over two and a half octaves, beginning on the G below the bass clef. It is written in treble clef and, therefore, is written a major thirteenth above the sounding, or concert, pitch. This instrument could be considered the *bass instrument* of the family.

Overall in the woodwind family, the clarinet family could be considered to be the *tenor* family of instruments, as these instruments are most often used within the orchestra.

The Saxophones

The **saxophone subgroup** has within it instruments ranging from soprano to bass. The saxophone family differs in timbre from the clarinet family in that the instruments are made of metal. They are similar, however, in that they have the same type of single-reed mouthpiece design. The saxophones are the latest group to be developed within the woodwind family. They were intended to bridge the gap between the woodwind timbres and the brass timbres. They have not as yet found their way into the standard orchestral configuration of woodwinds and have, instead, developed a life of their own in jazz and commercial usage.

The B♭ **soprano sax** is the *highest-pitched instrument* of the family. It has a range of over two octaves beginning on the A♭, two ledger lines below the treble clef. It is written in the treble clef one whole step above the concert pitch.

The E♭ **alto sax** is the *alto instrument* of the family and has a range of over two and a half octaves beginning on the D♭ within the bass clef. It is written in the treble clef, an interval of a major sixth above the concert pitch.

The B♭ **tenor sax** is the *tenor instrument* of the family and possesses a range of over two and a half octaves beginning on the A♭ in the bottom of the bass clef. It is written in the treble clef up a major ninth interval from the concert pitch.

The E♭ **baritone sax** is the *baritone instrument* of the family, even though it is mostly used as the bottom of any saxophone grouping. It has a range of over two and a half octaves beginning on the C two ledger lines below the bass clef. It is written in the treble clef a major thirteenth up from the concert pitch.

The B♭ **bass sax** is occasionally used in live performance of saxophone chamber music or in some recording sessions. It is not, however, regularly used because of its size and expense. The bass sax has a range of two and a half octaves beginning on the A♭ below the baritone sax's range. It is also written in the treble clef two octaves and a whole step above the concert pitch.

All of the saxophones, as well as many of the woodwinds, have either the exact or similar fingering for the instruments. Professional sax players, therefore, "double," or are expected to play more than one woodwind instrument. A varying degree of doubling ability between players is common, however.

THE DOUBLE REEDS

The **double reeds** of the woodwind family each possess the same type of sound production. The instrument is played through a mouthpiece created from two cane reeds loosely attached together in such a manner that air passes through these reeds, causing them to vibrate against each other.

The Oboes

The **oboes** are the *alto instruments* of the woodwind family. The two most frequently used members of this subgroup are the oboe and the English horn.

The oboe is the *soprano instrument* of the two and has a range of over two and a half octaves beginning on the B♭ below the staff of the treble clef. It is written in in the treble clef, in concert pitch or where it actually sounds.

The **English horn** is the *tenor instrument* of the two and has a range of two and a half octaves beginning on the E in the staff of the bass clef. It is written in the treble clef up a Perfect fifth interval.

The Bassoons

The **bassoon subgroup** includes the bassoon and the contrabassoon.

The **bassoon** has a range of over two and a half octaves beginning on the B♭, two ledger lines below the bass-clef staff. It is written in concert pitch, in the bass clef, for the low register up to the F above the bass-clef staff, and in the tenor clef, from there upward. The bassoon is the *soprano instrument* of this subgroup.

The *bass instrument* of this subgroup is the **contrabassoon**, which is pitched one octave lower than the bassoon and is written in a similar manner.

The Keyboard Instruments

The **keyboard instruments** include those instruments that use a keyboard for the entering of musical information. This entered data is then made into sound through either the channeling of air through a network of materials designed to carry air to an appropriate pipe or reed, the striking of a felt hammer against a string or string series, or the plucking of the string through some mechanism.

The **pipe organ** is the keyboard that generates its sound through the use of air and pipes. These instruments are specifically built for each space that houses them and they are designed to have a wide variety of sound timbres.

The **Allen organ** is the electronic version of the pipe organ. Through electronic circuitry, it attempts to make a more affordable alternative to the pipe organ. The Allen Company manufactured the first electronic organ of this nature and, therefore, has its name used synonymously with this overall category of instrument, even though there are now several manufacturers of these electronic organs.

The **piano** is now, and has been for many years, the standard acoustic keyboard. It comes in various sizes from nine-foot concert grands to smaller studio, upright models. The quality of this instrument differs from size to size and from manufacturer to manufacturer.

Another keyboard instrument still in use today is the **harpsichord**, a predecessor of the modern piano. The harpsichord is more limited in range than the piano and has a metallic, biting timbre. It generates its sound through the plucking of the individual strings. This plucking of the strings gives the instrument a more percussive character.

THE HARP   The **harp**, although not a keyboard instrument, is a predecessor of the piano. The piano can be likened to a harp that uses hammers instead of fingers. The harp is one of the oldest instruments; its cousins date back to pre-Biblical times. Today, the harp has strings, in various lengths, attached to a frame which allows them to hang freely. Pedals attached to the instrument act as muting devices so that chords and other specific tone groupings may be allowed to ring without unwanted tones. The harp is played primarily with the fingers and it may play melodic or harmonic material, or material used as special effects.

All of the instruments within this family are extremely demanding on the performer with regard to their preparation and training.

Fretted Instruments

The **fretted-instrument family** is related to the string-instrument family. Fretted instruments differ in size, construction, string materials, and string numbers. The most obvious difference between these families is the presence of *frets* along the neck of the fretted-instrument group. These **frets** are raised bars at regular intervals along the neck of the instrument on which the strings lie. They provide a point of reference with regard to the pitch being played. The performer of a string-family instrument, having no frets, is forced to make a very educated guess as to exactly where any particular note lies on the neck of the instrument. Through the use of frets, the guesswork is taken out; but in most cases more strings are added to the instrument, thus allowing even more versatility.

The members of this category of instruments are large and the timbres that are possible from them are numerous. This is one of the reasons that the instruments within this family are among the most popular in recent decades. A partial listing of instruments that fit into this category are: the **six-string guitar**, the **twelve-string guitar**, the **dobro**, the **mandolin**, the **four-string** (or **tenor**) **banjo**, the **five-string banjo**, the **six-string acoustic folk guitar**, the **Spanish guitar**, the **solid-body electric guitar**, the **hollow-body jazz guitar**, the **ukelele**, the **electric bass guitar**, the **electric five-string bass**, the **electric six-string bass**, the **fretless bass**, the **sitar**, and the **acoustic guitar-shaped Mexican mariachi bass**.

The Voice Family

The voice family is the family of instruments that comes from the human body itself. The range of the vocal instruments varies according to the timbre of each person's voice, but may be divided into four generic categories: *soprano, alto, tenor,* and *bass.*

The **bass** group is male and has a usual range of E below the bass-clef staff or lower, depending on the individual, up to middle C or higher, also depending on the individual. Music written for the bass voice will be found in the bass clef, in concert pitch.

The **tenor** group, too, is almost always male in gender and has a range of C, an octave below middle C, to the G above middle C or higher. Music for the tenor is written in the treble clef, an octave higher than concert pitch.

The **alto** voice is usually female, but it can be a young male, not yet gone through puberty. Males over the age of puberty who still sing in this register, are referred to as **castrati tenors**. The practice of castration of males in order to preserve the vocal range has died out in most of the world, but some literature may refer to this timbre. The range of the alto is from the G below middle C, to the E at the top of the treble-clef staff, or higher. It is written in the treble clef, in concert pitch.

The **soprano** voice is female and has a range from roughly middle C to A at the top of the treble-clef staff, or higher. It sounds in concert pitch and is written in the treble clef.

PROJECTS

1. Pick a sixteen-bar phrase of music that you have written. Orchestrate this phrase in ten different ways, using various instrumental colors and combinations.

21
Electronic Orchestration

Throughout the last two decades, there has been an explosion of electronic technology. As it applies to the music industry, it has made the use of electronic machinery affordable for the creative public and more user-friendly. It has brought with it an age of sound possibilities and timbre choices unequaled in the history of Western music.

Technology and the Musician

It has also placed more of a burden upon the individual musician with regard to the amount of specialized information and skills necessary for effective use of the technology to its fullest extent. To function creatively using the new technology, a composer or performer must not only be comfortable working within the parameters of acoustic orchestration, but also be capable of working with computers, operating sequencers, manipulating music-writing software, editing sound waves, programming analog and digital synthesizers, sampling existing sound waves, recombining these through MIDI components, and mixing, panning, recording, storing, coloring, and equalizing these sounds, using a mountain of outboard gear. The payoff for the individual within this nightmare of circuitry is the luxury of producing a finished usable work of quality, without having to depend on a busload of supporting musicians and technicians. The drawback to all of this is that the quality of the finished product is now more dependent than ever upon the creative and imaginative capacity of the composer/producer/programmer/artist and his or her individual degree of musicianship. Therefore, it is vital for the perpetuation of quality craftsmanship that today's music-industry student be trained thoroughly in the new skills as well as, and not instead of, the traditional skills.

Synthesizers

There are numerous manuals on the subject of sound synthesis and MIDI technology. These manuals vary according to each synthesizer manufacturer, and its products' mode of operation. They are usually included with the instrument upon its purchase. The scope of this subject is well beyond this text. However, a mention of what is possible may help build some confidence in the subject.

ANALOG
SYNTHESIZERS

This group of synthesizers was created first. **Analog synthesizers** produce a sound through an **oscillator**, which creates sound waves. All sounds have corresponding wave shapes, which can be grouped together in categories of similar wave shapes or patterns. The oscillators can be programmed to manufacture certain wave shapes, which can then be altered and colored through an enormous number of mathematical processes and combined with other wave shapes that are generated from the multiples of oscillators within the instrument. The analog synthesizer, then, is an instrument that allows you to create your own unique sound by actually constructing and editing it from standard sound-wave forms.

DIGITAL
SYNTHESIZERS

The **digital synthesizer** works on a similar principle as the analog synthesizer, but uses *digital circuitry* as its primary component to accomplish these functions.

Sampling

Sampling is the process of recording any sound, acoustic or electronic, by translating the sound into numbers, thereby storing the sound digitally into a computer's memory. The sound is played back electronically by activating that digital sequence. Many synthesizers now use sampled sounds as the basis for their sound banks. This synthesizer creates no sound of its own; it primarily plays back the sounds stored within it.

Sequencing

The act of sequencing refers to the storing of digital information within a computer. This information will be executed by the sequencer in rigid order or in sequence. In other words, you store MIDI information into the sequencer. This MIDI information tells the synthesizers or any other electronic MIDI gear when to start and stop their function. A sequencer then serves as the conductor of the electronic orchestra. The sequencer is programmed to do what you tell it to do.

Effects

There are many different ways to color the electronic signal further once it leaves the synthesizer or guitar. This process will alter the signal that those instruments generate through the processes of phasing, chorusing, equalizing, gating, and adding reverberation before that signal gets either to tape or amplifier. This field of outboard gear is constantly expanding and can provide endless possibilities of sound coloration.

Concepts in Electronic Orchestration

Through synthesizer and sampling technology, new sounds never before heard or sounds that approximate existing timbres can be created and made available to the palette of the orchestrator/composer/performer. As a general rule, it is best to maintain the integrity of the timbre of each sound that is within the palette. Whenever possible, *use the truest timbre available instead of one that only serves as an imitation of an acoustic timbre.*

Electronics can serve as an expansion and an addition to the palette of timbres; it functions best when woven into the fabric of the whole, supporting and coloring in its own unique way.

PROJECTS

1. Pick the same sixteen-bar phrase that you used in the projects section of Chapter 20. Orchestrate the same phrase five different ways, using only electronic timbres.

2. Use the same phrase of music and combine both acoustic and electronic timbres in five different ways, creating more possibilities.

Appendix
Interviews

Interview
with
Gino Vannelli

Montreal-born Gino Vannelli has had an extremely successful, seventeen-year career as a singer/songwriter/record producer. In addition, he has established a new record label—Vie Records.

His career is notable for artistic innovation through the endless search for better emotional communication. Vannelli's songs have been influenced by a variety of philosophies. For example, "Rhythm of Romance" on his album, *Inconsolable Man*, draws from the teachings of Albert Camus and of Zen Buddhism. Vannelli writes of the uncertainty and confusion of modern life as a wall that we create for ourselves and are afraid to go through. Once we do, however, it disappears, and we find it never really existed except in our own creation. While including themes that hold meaning for him, Vannelli encourages his listeners to seek out their own personal interpretations of his songs.

Vannelli's accomplishments are many including:

A Grammy nomination for "Powerful People" [1974], a Grammy nomination for Best Pop Performance for "I Just Want To Stop" [1978], five consecutive Juno Awards as Canada's Number One Male Singer, a Grammy nomination for Single of the Year for "Black Cars" [1985], two Grammy nominations for Male Vocalist of the Year [1986 and 1987], winner, along with brother Joe, of Recording Engineer of the Year [1987], and a nomination, with Joe, for Producer of the Year [1987].

His hit singles include:

"Living Inside Myself" [1981], gold-selling single (and platinum album) "Black Cars" [1985], and "Wild Horses" [1987].

His albums include:

Crazy Life [1973], *Powerful People* [1974], *Storm at Sunup* [1975], *Gist of the Gemini* [1976], *A Pauper in Paradise* [1977], *Brother to Brother* [1978], *Nightwalker* [1981], *Black Cars* [1985], *Big Dreamers Never Sleep* [1987], and *Inconsolable Man* [1991].

CG

GV

CG: *What is your background in regard to musical training?*

GV: I had percussion lessons from the ages of 12 to 16 or 17, some theory lessons. My father was a singer and most of my influence and training came from ear training, just listening very heavily to many kinds of music.

CG: *Your brothers work with you regularly, is that true?*

GV: Joe works with me on a full-time basis and Ross works with me once in a while.

CG: *What is their training?*

GV: Joe had keyboard training.

CG: *Are you a pianist as well?*

GV: I write all my songs on piano and guitar. I picked it up just looking at Joe, just dashing around on the piano myself, and picked up chords on the guitar.

CG: *I've been listening to your stuff for quite a long time and I have been influenced by it, but what was always intriguing about it*

*was—the contents of your lyrics seem to be so different than any-
body else's in that they are real-life topics that don't seem to be
commercially oriented with regard to a formula that is going to be
successful on the radio. It seems that it has had a lot of unique
integrity that has always worked. Can you talk to me about what
makes you choose a topic to write about?*

GV: Well, I think in the beginning many things fuel our creativity. And
most of the time it's things that upset our hearts and things that
we're madly searching for, and it's usually this feeling of discom-
fort with ourselves and ourselves in relationships and perhaps in
contrast or perhaps just relating to the world. For me that's been
the main source of creative lyrical energy. I've always had many
questions and too few answers to back them up and the only thing
I could do was basically just have diarrhea of the mouth. Just sit
down and just blab away and just think about it, think about it,
and fortunately for me there have been things that have been on
some people's minds too and not only my mind. So that, in effect,
although it doesn't make it mainstream, does make it accessible to
perhaps more of a limited amount of people, but it does make it
accessible.

CG: *Is your artistic goal to be successful in a broad sense or just to
fulfill your own passions and for whomever likes that, that's
wonderful, or . . . ?*

GV: Faced with the fact that you do make a living from what you do,
from being an artist, so that in a sense taints the artistry and in a
sense motivates it to go to places that perhaps you wouldn't go
otherwise. For instance, if you add a color to one color, the con-
stancy is yellow, if you add a green to it you get a certain color, or
if you add a blue to it you get another color. So the constant is
your desire to create, but if you add a little bit of willingness to
make a living at it, well, then, it does something to it and then
perhaps you add the color of wanting to prove yourself creatively
or wanting to do something that no one's done before or whatever
the reason is, it completely shades the constant which is your
artistry, which is the basic medium you work with. So my inten-
tions have never been to be mainstream, but although admittedly I
make a living doing this so I always have to be conscious of the
fact that there has to be a certain amount of people that have to
share my experience out there in order for me to keep on doing

this to make a living. As far as a conscious choice to be mainstream, it's never really been a conscious choice of mine to be mainstream; and even when I've tried it, I've not been very successful or very good at it—but I have done it successfully, inadvertently. Some songs I've just released have become hits for me not because I really tried; it just happened to be the songs were right at the time.

CG: *You've changed a lot over the years as far as the bed, not the lyrical content—the bed and the production value of the songs have really transformed a lot over the years. I got out* Crazy Life *and put it on the stereo the other day, and I was amazed at the cleanness of it all and how wonderfully perfect each setting was and how thoughtful it was. If that were to be released now, how odd it would be. To what degree do you make choices in your production decisions?*

GV: Technology influences. Technology is a language you use. So inspiration and creativity are sort of like the white light. It could be anything, but it does serve as the fuel. Then, perhaps, the white light defuses into particular colors, depending upon where it seeks to go, and so technology is sort of the bed that it chooses to lie in at that particular time. The technology dictates in what direction the creativity will go. For instance, when electrical instruments started coming out, a lot of people started writing their songs around the electrical instruments. Rock-and-roll is specifically rock-and-roll because of electrical instruments. You really couldn't do rock-and-roll if you had to just have a piano and a string bass and a drum, not the way we know it today. What made rock-and-roll more feasible was the guitar, especially the electric guitar. Electric bass came out. People started miking drums, kick drum, and so on and so forth. Whereas the prevailing technology of the symphony orchestra was the string instruments, and so forth, so people wrote their pieces with that in mind. As technology moves along, changes, progresses, whatever it does, as a writer or a person who chooses to create, you're always trying to, in a sense, milk it for all that its worth and try to create new sounds that will again further inspire you to dig deeper. So, in the last few albums we've employed computer technology, sampling technology, and so on and so forth, and better studio technology, like most artists have done to further our interests and to keep going.

CG: *That brings up a question: to what degree does technology color your creativity as far as topic matter, and how does that influence what tunes you do?*

GV: The technology sometimes inspires you to come up with something, but songs that are inspired by technology are definitely not songs that are really usually written from the heart. Songs that are written from the heart usually have, for me, a local content that is really the bedrock of the song. Then some chord changes along with melody line that I think are good enough to make this thing into a song. Very rarely have I been inspired for more than one or two songs here and there to write a song because of a sound or because of a way of doing things. But, for instance, if I do decide on the next album, I'd like to get a quartet together or a trio, and I'd like the instruments to sound like this or sound like that; then that will influence what songs I do use and what songs I do write. I wouldn't write a grandiose song with lots of parts and things for a trio; I'd try to make it more intimate.

CG: *So you write per project, per album?*

GV: In a sense. When artists in the old days used to write for the string quartet, they'd write a piece that would perhaps be a little bit more refined, a little busier in certain sections, a little more counterpoint, a little more "chatty" here and there. And then, when they'd write a piece for the biggest symphony orchestra, they'd have more pads, a slow movement here and there 'cause you couldn't have a hundred guys doing solo instrument parts. So the medium changes; so therefore, you have to adjust to the medium.

CG: *I've always followed your drummers, especially in the early albums, the first six or so. You've always had great drummers and the feels that were chosen really allowed them to play. Has there been an intention to do it that way?*

GV: Yes, I was a percussionist, a drummer. [I] played drums on the first album and also some cuts on the *Black Cars* album, so I've always been very conscious of great drumming and I've always appreciated it, and I think it has always helped me to elevate what I do to a higher standard.

CG: *When I think of your music, I think of innovation. One of my favorite albums is* A Pauper In Paradise, *because of the style and lyrics done with (Don) Sebesky. To do a whole half of an album like that is wonderful. How did that come about?*

GV: Not many artists get that opportunity to do it today.

CG: *What made you decide to do that?*

GV: This sort of madness in me to experience music thicker and richer and bigger and deeper. I had done stuff on the *Storm at Sunup* album, orchestral stuff with synthesizers, and I took it a little farther with the *Gist of the Gemini* album. Synthesizers couldn't give me what I wanted to do, so the whole symphony really became an outlet for my personal expression. I needed to do it. I paced up and down and wondered if I should do it, if I shouldn't, and when I decided to do it, it all fell into place very quickly. As far as the band, we took the band and we rehearsed the third movement with the band, and it was just a strange kind of planning.

CG: *All three of those albums are real interesting, and the formal concept, the whole suite kind of concept—it has a classical kind of form to it. Are there influences that made you want to do that? I think that those three albums are really innovative for that style. Is there room for that kind of thing now?*

GV: I think so. I would do it differently and my topics would be something new and fresh that I could sink my teeth into. Everything's changing so rapidly and nothing's carved in stone. I'd like to go back to doing that, and on the other hand, I'd like to experience some things I haven't done yet. I'd like to work with a jazz trio maybe, or quartet, and write a whole album with that feel too. I've never experienced that. The unknown is always the most exciting. I don't discount the fact that I'd like to experiment with the orchestra and orchestral sounds in the future, but I feel that I've done a lot of that. Perhaps in the future I could experiment a little more with something different. As far as all that stuff, that stuff was really writing for the medium. When I knew that we could do certain things with synthesizers, the drummers could give me certain things, then I would push it, push the threshold as hard and as deep as I could. With the symphony orchestra in England, the Royal Philharmonic, some of the parts were difficult for them to play with the band in the third movement, but with a little effort we managed it. You're really limited by the medium. Sometimes I heard stuff in my head that could not be accomplished—they were too much or too fast, and by the time you got them down they were just muddled.

CG: *Well, you had one of the finest arrangers living working with you and if it couldn't be done, it couldn't be done.*

GV: Don Sebesky?

CG: *Right.*

GV: Yeah, he's wonderful.

CG: *Your synthesizer work—what I've always found intriguing about it is the way you used it. It's not so much for color or trick—it's an orchestral instrument in itself that has an integral part and reason for being there. You seem to be one of the few who use it in this manner.*

GV: Well, yes, it was always important to me to use it in such a manner. It is an instrument—well, the synthesizer itself is a generic term, but every synthesizer has its own unique sound and it can be turned into a speaking voice. Synthesizers are still very, very important because they alone can give you certain textures and certain things that can create sounds and feels and ambiences that other things cannot give you.

CG: *To what degree do you feel closed in as far as the business end of making a hit and feeling the confines of formulas—versus thinking in terms of artistry, which is above the mainstream formulas? How do you adapt to that?*

GV: Well, you have to take your bumps and you have to understand at one point that if you choose to do certain things, you must expect the commensurate results. You can't do things like the *Gist of the Gemini* or *A Pauper in Paradise* and expect to sell two million albums. It can always happen, but there's no reason to expect it. The audience that is turned on by certain things usually aren't audiences that are in the millions. So it's no sacrifice at all, but it's a sacrifice from the point that you don't expect to retire from making an album like *A Pauper in Paradise.* What you expect to do is to divulge yourself of something that is within yourself. It is to free yourself of something that keeps haunting you. And that to me is something, a much richer reward. As far as the new stuff, some of the new stuff was done a little more mainstream, but still isn't exactly mainstream. What I'm learning too is, as long as you are logical and understand that there is always going to be a proportionate reward to what you're doing, and don't expect more and don't expect less, then it's ok. I'm prepared to live with an album that doesn't get past number 50 or doesn't even enter the charts at all, and just sells enough for me to make another album.

CG: *Isn't that diametrically opposed to the thinking of a large record company that expects to make hits?*

GV: Yes!

CG: *How do you walk the fine line of business in keeping them happy and doing what you want to do?*

GV: I've always had enough chart success to keep me alive. With the last two albums, *Black Cars* did very well for me internationally and the last album, *Big Dreamers Never Sleep*, did good enough for me internationally. I had one international hit that was top ten in seven or eight countries—not this country, so a lot of people don't know about it. It was one of those songs that came, and it was a natural song, and it happened. One of the ways that I'm working around this is I have my own record company now that my album is coming out on. This latest album is called *Inconsolable Man*, and it's on Vie Records, and it's distributed by BMG. So I consider myself extremely fortunate to be able to have the opportunity to put out my own album distributed by a reputable distribution firm, and if it sells just well enough for me to make another one, that's fine for me. I think it was a writer who said, "Too much success is really bad for the artistic mind, too little is too depressing," so somewhere in between is good. It keeps the longing, it keeps the hunger, and it keeps you searching. Perhaps it's a relative statement, but for me all the peaks and valleys, commercially, of my career have always pushed me to keep doing it, and keep doing it until I realize it's part of my being.

CG: *Who is your audience, demographically?*

GV: It's hard to say. I can't really say it's this or it's that.

CG: *I know there are certain pockets of cultism, so to speak. New Orleans seems to be a hotbed for you.*

GV: That's what it is when you're a bit of a cult hero. You go to certain towns, people idolize what you do, and you go to other towns and people just could care less. That's ok, though; it comes with the territory. I've been fortunate enough to have a solid enough audience that supports what I do. I've been doing it for seventeen years.

CG: *What did you listen to when you were young? What music helped create your language and your sense of intuition? What do you listen to now?*

GV: I listened to practically everything that Western culture had to offer from the symphonic to Latin to rock and to jazz—big band. It really is Western music that I listen to. I'm becoming more interested in Eastern music.

CG: *What about it?*

GV: The sound, the feel, and the tonal things that the Indians use. The Indian flute is very different, it could play in quarter- and half-tones, for a flute it's very interesting. Also some of the Japanese stuff, some of the Buddhist mantras are actually quite hard to accomplish. What I'm saying is that music is not just Western now for me. I'm trying to listen to more. I'm just entering a phase now where I need to listen and want to listen to what's being done as much as possible around the whole planet.

CG: *You must have had a good support base when you were a kid as far as cultural listening and awareness of things. You can't just do the* Gist of the Gemini *out of nothing.*

GV: Yes, symphonic and contemporary rock really influenced that, and the jazz element that really brought in something that nobody was really doing at the time.

CG: *I've always looked at you with those three albums as almost a third-stream type of thing for rock, like the classical and jazz third-stream people were doing. You did that for a while.*

GV: And I really got it out of me. I really had it going within me for many years and it came out and I'm just changing at this point. I'm in my late thirties—I'm 38 years old now—and life means something different to me now. I've got a son four years old and life takes on new meaning. You search for new meaning in music, and it's not just being able to prove that you know how to do something. It's perhaps a gentler side that I'm trying to accomplish or perhaps a deeper thing that I'm trying for in maybe not so much instrumentation, but it's in my voice now. So my concentration in the last few years has been a bit scattered, only to find itself settling in one place that seems to be developing focus at this point.

CG: *When you have an idea, hypothetically, if you're going to do the next project with the jazz quartet and that's the focus, how would you go about writing and what decisions would you make?*

GV: The first thing I would do is to scout the country to find a quartet that would be a unit that I'd like to work with—or put one together that would be really excellent and just play with them and watch them play, watch the piano player, watch the bass player, see if I can employ his technique. I might have a few songs in mind, see if they would fit; if not, maybe write a few more. Allow myself to be open. Allow myself to accept the fact that I don't know something, that I could learn.

CG: *That's interesting.*

GV: With the overriding confidence that I would be able to take it in and with practice and understanding and a little bit of self-love, accomplish it and be able to write for their musicianship. That's one aspect; another would be to listen. Keep listening to stuff that I don't quite understand or stuff that is beyond me so I keep reaching. The act of reaching is the sincere act of wanting. Keep that desire at peak level, 'cause once desire starts turning to smoke or dust, you have nothing. Those are a couple of ways. Then perhaps to go in the studio and just horse around a little bit and come up with things and say, "This is a very good direction; I'd like to take the whole project in this direction"—or perhaps, "I haven't found it yet . . .", or . . .

CG: *Do you have an overall concept for your albums?*

GV: Yes, of course.

CG: *So they're all pieces of a whole that build to a certain point—or just a snapshot kind of thing?*

GV: Well, no. When I had the group together and we did the *Powerful People* album, there was a sound to that album, an approach. That sound and approach was developed during rehearsal by hand-picking certain musicians, so on and so forth. Same thing with *Storm* and *Gist of the Gemini* and then when I worked with the orchestra and all, I had that concept in mind. So if I would have a concept in mind to do an Eastern type sound album, I would pick musicians that would be more akin to such playing. You must point in a direction. There's an old saying that says, "Nature unaided is completely worthless," to humans at least. You take basic energy or basic influences and point it in directions. You have to put it in a direction, and then things follow through. You give it form, you give it content. As human beings we don't understand pure energy. We understand energy as it is transformed into something cohesive, something conscious, something intelligent. How intelligent, how inclusive, how aggressive depends upon the vision of the visionary.

CG: *Compositionally, form is very important. How do you go about not necessarily creating, but uncovering the form that the piece is going to take?*

GV: Well, it's an experiment. You know, you sit down; you might come up with something on the piano that's just a nice melody and a nice lyric, maybe it's half done; and as you're playing with musicians, you say, "Try this." Because of the strength of a bass player or a drummer's strength, "I like the way you do that, play this beat." Then I give him a couple of changes to play with what I've written at home and see if it feels right. Then all of a sudden, it gives me ideas to expand the song. It may happen that way or it just may happen sitting down at the piano and I just have a flash—and I start writing or rewriting something until it's complete and it's just a basic generic song with an interesting or complete lyric to it—and as I take it to a band, I change it. I change its beat, I turn it around. I do this to it, perhaps change some changes; it's never really done 'til it's done.

CG: *Does the lyric lead you to a different section of the music? Do you think lyrically and melodically at the same time?*

GV: I think the lyric content is more and more important to me. I find no reason to write a song unless I have something that I feel at the time is interesting to say.

CG: *When you have a flash, does it come together as melody and lyric at the same time—or is it one or the other?*

GV: Well, some songs melodically support as if you're supporting some-one doing a handstand or supporting someone on your shoulders. The music just supports the lyric, which is the light of the song, which is the integral part of the song. Some artists have shown that to be an interesting way, a unique way of writing and have been very successful as artists, namely Dylan, and so on, and so forth. Some artists have a little bit more technical capability—so with a little more musical ability, a little more complexity in the music, the complexity of the lyric, the lyrics had to be etched a little bit be-cause lyrics are not the sole creative force—the music is. So the lyrics sometimes must, I can't say suffer, but they have to accom-modate the music sometimes. Because the melody's so great, if you want to say, "If you really want me"; but you can't say it so you have to say, "If you want me." So sometimes you have to let whatever's most important to you take precedent. And to the other extreme where music is so important, people just use their lyrics as support for their melodies and rhythms. So it depends on where the slant is, you know. I'm talking about from the composi-tional aspect. I'm not talking about from the performance or the emotion aspect at all. Because many times we have songs that aren't songs at all, but are interesting productions, but still have artistic value. I mean a lot of the songs of the big bands, you know you take very simple songs and just either complicate them or em-bellish them so that they became interesting. So we can do the same thing in the studio, but I'm talking just a compositional value. There's always a stress on something. If the stress is on the whole entire package, a melody with form and a cohesive interesting lyric, you'll find that there's an art to balancing the two. If the stress is solely on the lyric, then you'll find melodies that just support the lyric. If the stress is solely on the music, you'll find lyrics that basically support the melody.

CG: *Can you write without thinking orchestrally or orchestrationally?*

GV: Yes. I've written some pretty simple songs along the way.

CG: *So that's a whole stage in itself, to arrange it, produce it?*

GV: Yeah.

CG: *What decisions do you make at that level? When you get something that works lyrically, melodically, and formally on a page and you want to come to life with it, what decisions do you make there?*

GV: Well, you have to understand that it's usually written with a vision. As I'm writing, I usually hear the way it should be on record. So that initial vision gets you to a place where you say, "Let me do this, let me use this instrument, I hear it this way," and then you may go into the studio and your vision didn't exactly work and then you make repairs and modifications. And then that's where my brother Joe or Ross or someone in the studio might say, "Well, it would be better if we took it this tempo or I didn't play at all on this." Or maybe you should take the song and change the arrangement. Sometimes a song comes to life or dies a slow death with the right or wrong arrangement.

CG: *Do you do all that yourself or have you ever, outside of the Sebesky situation, brought in someone else?*

GV: Most of it myself with Joe.

CG: *It's a very complex thing to talk to kids about and I sit looking at their work and see basic problems; yet, there's sometimes some real inspiration there. It's more uncovering form and structure than putting it in there, I feel.*

GV: Well, my deep advice to kids is that they have to learn about form, and form means an education. You can't just listen to music—you have to have some formal background, an understanding of the basics of the laws; and if you want to break them or use them or whatever. If you just listen to three-chord rock-and-roll, if you just listen to the music that is contemporary music, you're already taking music that's been filtered, in a sense, or watered down, in a sense. You can't just take what's been already handed down to you third generation. You must go to the source. Most of what we're doing in music has its sources in classical and jazz and older pop music. If you listen to that and you have a basic understanding of that, it gives you a better understanding of writing more interesting material. Some of our best composers today—whether it be Paul Simon, Don Henley, or Sting or Peter Gabriel—have a good understanding of older material, older jazz stuff, older pop stuff. They have a good understanding of form. Now, to just simply listen, say, to Peter Gabriel and say, "Well, I'm going to do what he does and I'm a new kid," you'll get something that's maybe almost as good, but not as good. In other words, you must go to his point, his point of reference, and then if you want to emulate him artistically, you can do so; but it's not good enough just to go to his point because he's already been filtered, after listening to what he's been listening to. So the deeper you go, the better it is, that's what I'm saying, and a formal education helps that. It could also smother it if you use it solely as your guiding force. It must be something you imply. If a kid out there wants to be a contemporary composer I would suggest that he look at the best, compare himself to the best, and listen to who the best have listened to. An understanding of that particular form, I think, is integral. That's why people like Paul Simon could come back after ten years of not being popular and do stuff that is still good. Because he has a good understanding of music, of Gershwin, and so on and so forth. He's always talked about it. He has also an excellent understanding of poetry, rhyme and reason, form and lyric. That gives him fuel. It gives him food. It gives him extra water in the well. But when the well periodically runs dry, all he has to do is wait and it will replenish because his background has been richer. So the more you listen to, the more you have to choose from.

CG: *That brings up an interesting thought. When kids are cutting their teeth and learning to play, as well as to write and to listen, of course you get into a whole time period of years for some people, of learning styles, of style analysis, and copping licks, and transcribing stuff, and doing cover tunes, and all this which is cutting your teeth; but it's almost a double-edged sword, good and bad, in that the good is you begin to learn a language, the bad is that many people never get to the point where they quit doing other people's stuff and cross the bridge to find themselves as to where they want to go. Do you have any advice on—because you're very original—how to have the faith to expect yourself to have your own voice and to go ahead and follow it?*

GV: You're not only talking about a condition of music and musicians, you're talking about a condition of life. Most people will not wear something unless it's fashionable. Most people will not wear their hair in a certain way unless it's fashionable. Most people will not say things unless they are things generally accepted by the public at large. What I'm trying to say is, originality is not something that you choose, it chooses you. All of a sudden, you wake up one day and you say, "You know what, I don't feel like the other people feel. I really and truly admire this guy and that guy, and I love this musician and love the way that Eric Clapton used to play and dah dah, dah dah, dah dah." Then you say, "But, everytime I come to do it, I don't hear it that way, I hear it this way." And if you're ready to reconcile yourself with that, that's your first step. But a lot of people, they just want to sort of be in there, and be accepted, and do what the basic mainstream is doing. And if that's what they want, that's perfectly fine.

CG: *And that's what the great ones did.*

GV: Well, what makes a great man or what makes a great musician is not always great circumstances. Many great people have come from deprivation and difficult backgrounds—a yearning in their gut that they can't really explain, and it's a very complicated issue. But the point is that it is not something desirable from a way-of-life standpoint, but it is something desirable definitely from a creative standpoint. Most musicians I know who are original suffer the pangs of being original. Because in a sense they can never really be like anybody else. They have their way of doing it—and when they have great years, they are highly idolized; but as they're being idolized, their head is already five years ahead. So they can't really sit and eat and walk in the confection and rice.

CG: *It's a very scary place to be.*

GV: Yes, it is. It's a very isolated place, and the only thing that does give you any kind of comfort is the fact that you are doing it and you keep doing it. Perhaps for me, it leads to undoubted deep spiritual thinking and deep spiritual searching because it's almost an unbearable feeling to live with. Because we are basically gregarious and social animals by nature, we do at one point want to feel like we're part of the bunch; but part of us hates that. So you have to come to terms with that, and the only way to do it is sometimes to go on searching a little bit deeper.

CG: *The classical and jazz fields have always had their people who have followed their own drummers and ways of thinking, and many of them are heroes and cult figures who have their own stories; but they're celebrated as pivotal people. Beethoven's like that. Stravinsky's like that. Charlie Parker's like that. Rock-and-roll or pop doesn't seem to be as fertile a bed to inspire uniqueness as those other fields.*

GV: Well, there are people not at the front, where people make a living at it; it's not as elite, you have to understand something. It's easy to take people like Beethoven and Franz Liszt, you know we have about maybe fifty composers that we always turn to. I am sure between the sixteenth and nineteenth century, Europe produced thousands of composers . . .

CG: *That's right! Many of whom were more famous in their day than those we celebrate today.*

GV: That's right. Going back to the original question, originality. We all are original in the sense that we are all cut from heaven in our own unique way. As to whether we choose to be outwardly original in our expression is truly not really a matter many times of choice; it's a matter of just happening to be there and happening to be that person. I couldn't help where I was born. I was born in Montreal. My father was totally into music. Because of the cultural barrier, I never really felt terribly Americanized. So I liked to listen to more classical stuff. The only stuff that I thought was worth listening to was more complicated big band and jazz pianists and all that. Because of my language problem, when I was in my early teens, I spoke half French and half English, so I couldn't really master either one of them. So by the time I was sixteen I realized that I had to work really hard to master the English language or get even remotely close to mastering it. So its inevitable result was I read more, I plunged into the language any way that I could. And the result was that I became interested in the language and I started employing it in songs. Do you see what I'm trying to say? It's like we're born with a certain set of conditions that lead us to a very inevitable destiny.

CG: *Do you write in French?*

GV: No. I love the language from the standpoint that when I could still speak it in conversation.

CG: *Would the rhythm of a certain language change your thinking? I'm not bilingual myself, so I've never had that experience. I've known several bilingual people who say they have to stop and think and translate to themselves and find a simile. It's not exactly the same and I was just curious how that musically works out.*

GV: Everybody thinks in their own language, in their own native tongue.

CG: *Is there anything that you would like to add, to give to people, advice or encouragement?*

GV: Yeah. Remember the originality though, the certain set of potentials they were born with, is always just a potential, and they must live up to that potential. And if it's within them to live up to that potential, I say, "Go do it. It's worth the pain, it's worth a little bit of sacrifice. And don't be afraid of the pain because the pain will be twice as bad if you don't do it. If you're looking back on your life saying, 'I could have done this, I could have done that.'" It's better as you're young to plunge in, make the mistakes, be the fool, be anybody you need to be, but learn. Open your heart and delve deeply into it. Express yourself, learn the power of expression, because that very person may be the person who influences society at large in a positive way, in a good way, in an artistic, aesthetic way. Thank God for the last remaining artists in the music business that do see music that way. Because they keep the aesthetic value high. If we have no other God than a God of Aesthetics, this society would be twice as good as it is. What I'm saying is that the problem with Western society or the problem with music today is not that there's a lack of artists, not that there's a lack of creativity, not that there's a lack of stuff that's at our disposal; what it is is the desires or obsessions are in the wrong place. Too much materialism, too much—at least to Western minds—success-oriented music. So it limits the culture, it limits our thought process, it limits willingness to open up ourselves to other cultures, to other people's way of thinking, to different sounds, and so on, and so forth. So it's one type of thinking that keeps accentuating the same kind of thinking. The only thing that gives it life is new blood and new thought, new culture, new desires. This country was not founded by people who just wanted to make a quick buck. This country was founded on ideals. And I'm saying that when music becomes founded solely on money, it loses its ideal. And when it loses its ideal, then it's a question of time before it degrades. Because it starts becoming a parody of itself. So hopefully, as cycles are, our next cyclical change would be that people, not only music, would be more inspired to breathe in life and accept a whole new challenge of life and see themselves and the planet in a whole different light. And that, of course, may be helped by music, but definitely should be reflected by music.

Interview
with
Dan Fogelberg

The stellar career of singer/songwriter/producer Dan Fogelberg is one that inspires adoration from faithful fans and spawns envy from industry competitors. A sensitive composer of many memorable songs, he is destined to be a force in the music industry for many years to come.

Fogelberg's hit singles include:

"Go Down Easy," "Language of Love," "Missing You," "Make Love Stay," "Hard to Say," "Leader of the Band," "Same Old Lang Syne," "Run for the Roses," "Longer," "Heart Hotels," "The Power of Gold," and "Part of the Plan."

His albums include:

The Wild Places (Full Moon/Epic) 1990; *Exiles* (Full Moon/ Epic) 1987; *High Country Snows* (Full Moon/Epic) 1985; *Windows And Walls* (Full Moon/Epic) 1984, certified Gold with sales of over 500,000; *Greatest Hits* (Full Moon /Epic) 1982, certified Platinum for sales over one million; *The Innocent Age* (Full Moon/Epic) 1981, Platinum; *Phoenix* (Full Moon/Epic) 1979, Platinum; *Twin Sons of Different Mothers* with Tim Weisberg (Full Moon/Epic) 1978, Platinum; *Nether Lands* (Full Moon/Epic) 1977, Platinum; *Captured Angel* (Full Moon/Epic) 1975, Platinum; *Souvenirs* (Full Moon /Epic) 1974, Platinum; and *Home Free* (Columbia) 1972, Gold.

Fogelberg gathers material for his songs from many sources. His most recent album, *The Wild Places*, draws from his own experiences and from the influences of well-known thinkers and artists such as Henry David Thoreau, Ansel Adams, Aaron Copland, John Lennon, and Georgia O'Keefe. He dedicates his songs to these people and to others who have had a great impact on the land, such as the Native Americans, whose traditions he admires, and the immigrants who settled America.

CG

DF

CG: *What do you think is important in the composition of a popular song? What goes into making something of worth instead of something that's trite?*

DF: Musically, lyrically, or overall?

CG: *Overall musical effect.*

DF: Even though it goes against the grain of contemporary pop music, I still believe that truth and intellectual honesty are very important in songwriting. I think that's what perhaps separates the singers/songwriters, who are recognized as such, from the pop writers, who are only writing for Top 40 radio, which is writing towards the largest common denominator. I believe that that integrity, and that honesty, and that depth of emotion, that ability to express a very deep emotion in a unique way, is the most important thing to me. I think the communication of the deep emotion in myself to one other person is the way you have to relate to it. You have to forget the overall scheme, the overall size of the audience, and just concentrate on reaching each person individually. I think if you succeed, if one person hears that record and it moves them for whatever reason, to tears, to happiness, to anger, whatever, if it stirs emotion and does more than make them want to tap their fingers and drive their cars, then I think you have succeeded in an artistic level other than just a pop-music level.

CG: *How do you go about that, personally, when you write? You do a lot of things that are autobiographical, in a sense?*

DF: Yeah, I have. I think in the past I've chosen to work a lot in an autobiographical vein. Obviously, to be intellectually honest, you can't be too distantly philosophical. I think it has to be a philosophy which is generated within yourself and within your own experience. If you're just regurgitating some dogmatic, religious, or philosophical viewpoint, that's not your particular experience. I think you have to work within the framework of your own particular experience and be as honest and truthful to that experience as you possibly can be, within the limitations of subjectivity.

CG: *You're a multitalented musician; you play keyboards and guitars. You also are a well-skilled craftsman in lyric writing. What decisions do you make that make you happy when you sit down to write, perform, and produce? How do you maintain a personal integrity?*

DF: I think that the most objective part is the songwriting. When I'm writing, that's a very personal, deep, and emotional experience. Afterwards, I have to become an objective observer on that particular song, as a producer or musician, and say, "OK, what's the best way to arrange this? What's the best way to produce this in the studio to get my idea across, and yet, to create a sonic environment for it that is not in any way detrimental?" The song, at that point, means very little to me. It is then something that I look at as a piece of art on a canvas. I have the ability to use any colors in my palette to express that song and to enhance that song, and therefore, to get it across better than just a pure emotional experience of one guitar and one voice, which is also very powerful. But in order to compete in the commercial marketplace, you have to produce, to an extent, records. Now I would love to see the recording industry go back to a simpler production, because I think we've gotten too over-produced, too slick, too machinated, that we're losing any sort of value of the lyrical content or the emotional count of the song. To me, I grew up in a tradition of blues and folk, and those songs were so incredibly powerful because they were so direct and so sparse.

CG: *They're very personal and very acoustic, too, in a day which is high-tech.*

DF: Yeah.

CG: *So, you do have to fight a battle when you produce a record—like in 1990,* The Wild Places—*about how you're going to orchestrate it?*

DF: Absolutely. Also, the business is so restrictive and so fickle these days, that you certainly do have to do a certain amount of nodding to contemporary production values which have evolved, I don't know how, through the evolution of technology. Music has become so technological, and the production of a record is almost more important than the song. In 99 percent of the cases on radio today, the song is the least of it. First of all, it's the production, which is very standardized. Second of all, it's the vocal performance. The lyrics mean nothing, the song means nothing, and the melody means nothing. I don't care for that. I still believe that the melody is something that is very spiritual and (a) sacred part of the song. And if it means as much to a person as the words do, if it's an original and it is married correctly to the lyrical content, then it becomes a very powerful statement.

CG: *Who are your influences musically, personally? Who did you grow up listening to and what has shaped your language?*

DF: There's so many. I think, lyrically, Gordon Lightfoot (and) Joni Mitchell. Probably those two more than anyone lyrically. Musically, I'd have to say The Beatles, The Buffalo Springfield, (and) Eric Clapton. Joni Mitchell has certainly has been an enormous influence, (Gordon) Lightfoot, Paul Simon. In recent years, I'd probably say Bruce Cockburn more than anybody. I think he's a magnificent writer.

CG: *What did you get lyrically out of those people?*

DF: I got their love of language and I think I got a certain sense of how to use internal rhyme so it's not stilted. I mean to use words that you wouldn't expect to hear. Most songwriters write very trite emotions. They're like Hallmark greeting cards. I have been accused of that myself from time to time, and I wouldn't altogether disagree. But, to always be searching for unusual word combinations and unusual sound combinations that stand out above the crowd. I always love it when I find a word that I've never used in a song, and I strive to (find) it in every song that I write. That is a new way of expressing it, a new, more concise way of saying it. If you can find a three- or four-syllable word that you've never used, well, that's like Scrabble, you get more points for that.

CG: *And musically, those influences. What did you borrow . . . ?*

DF: What did I get from them? Again, I think it's a sense of melody. I think those people that I mentioned were very original and very melodic, the Beatles especially. They did it so often and in such a short period of time. Their staying power and their pure creative power was awesome. Same with, I think, Buffalo Springfield, which I still consider the American Beatles. I think that was the most original American group that has ever been, with the exception of The Band, maybe. I like all those guys. The Springfield, I just thought, had a great melodic sense, but they also married a very innate American sense to it, just as The Beatles took the British sense. The Springfield married country-and-rock music and pop music and blues music in such an interesting way, and yet their melodies and their lyrics were always so incredibly original.

CG: *Your* Innocent Age *album, on the album credits it says "a song cycle," which is, frankly, a borrowed form from art music and a concept of (individual) units (within a whole collection) pertaining to one subject matter. Was that a conscious effort?*

DF: Yeah.

CG: *I thought that it came off wonderfully and it was a song cycle in every sense. Why did you choose to do it that way, and is there room for expansion of formal structure in popular music based on the confines of a consumer and his tastes, much like what we were just talking about with production values?*

DF: First of all, *The Innocent Age* didn't start as a song cycle. It just started as a bunch of songs that I found myself writing around the same subject matter, which was maturity. (It was) leaving your childhood behind and facing your adult years, which I think is a crisis in everyone's life. For me it was particularly intense. As I wrote the album, I actually had the thing all produced and ready to go. I was trying to sequence it and I only had two sides at that point. It was New Year's Eve, and I was alone that particular New

Year's Eve. I was struggling to put this album in some sort of context that would work for me, and as I did it, I realized that I hadn't said enough. At the same time I was still writing about this. So I said, "Look, like it or not, this is gonna have to be a double record and it's gonna have to be some sort of format to explain itself to an audience." I didn't want to write what they call a concept album because a concept album is basically fictional and it tells a story. This was an autobiographical series of, perhaps, philosophical recollections or reflections. So the song cycle seemed to be the only format that it really worked in. At that point, I had already issued "Same Old Lang Syne" to radio and the record company was saying, "Where's the album?" I said, "Sorry, it won't be for another six months." I went back in and cut sides three and four. I think it's more and more difficult as we go on because music is being so limited by radio. I think it's being so formatted that I don't know if there is much space (for expansion). And yet, there's always going to be aberration. I think good art will rise to the surface. Sting's new record is, if anything, a song cycle. I don't know if you know the work?

CG: *No, I haven't gotten it yet.*

DF: You should check it out. It's a fairly brilliant piece of work for this day and age. He's dealing with a lot of relationships with his father on this record, and with the sea. There's a recurring theme in all through his work, through the whole record. To me, its like a continuation from song to song, and it's been very successful; so I think there's still room for it, but it's the aberration rather than the norm. I also think there's very few people capable of sustaining it.

CG: *Well, it takes time to do that. A double record takes a concentrated effort to listen and get . . .*

DF: Yeah.

CG: *. . . an informational process over a period of time. Everyone is geared to a three-and-a-half minute attention span based on radio, which is incredibly sad . . .*

DF: It certainly is.

CG: *. . . for musicians to have to speak to an audience that has a response time of three minutes. I think (yours) is a real quality* *effort. I think that there's plenty of room for innovation in this area, but it takes some effort from the listener.*

DF: They're not willing to give that at this point. Radio, like it or not, is geared to (the) fourteen-year-old mind. It's not geared toward the 35-year-old or 40-year-old intellect.

CG: *Do you think that that will change as the median age changes?*

DF: I really don't, no. It's very frustrating these days. I think it's in the worst shape it's ever been in radio. There's not much room for any sort of intellect or any sort of real artistry on Top 40 radio. The ones that do break through are the exceptions, again. Like Henley's *The End of Innocence* was a really off-the-wall type of record. It really delivered a social criticism, a great melody, but those really are the exceptions anymore. I would love to see a change, but as long as the demographics remain the same, and that's who they're selling the acne cream to, and (who's) buying the Mustangs, then I don't think it's going to change. I think radio is becoming the arbiter for whatever the music business is. Since the music business is purely in the business of selling records and making money, I don't really think many record companies or radio stations could give a damn, to be honest with you, as long as their profit margins are there.

CG: *Do you think that popular music is an art form, versus a craft?*

DF: Do I? No, I really don't.

CG: *Do you think that it could be?*

DF: I think it could be and I think it has been.

CG: *What, in your mind, raises it from a craft to an art?*

DF: I think the songwriting. We had such a brilliant flash of songwriting in the late sixties and the seventies. There really were some great songwriters that surfaced. So far, in the eighties and nineties there have been none that I can see, very few. The ones that have are not young people; they're my age, that have just been struggling all those years. Like Shawn Colvin, who I think is a brilliant songwriter. But, she's been around as long as I have—just trying to get a break. I don't see many young people coming into the business—and that frightens me—that are picking up the slack for the Randy Newmans, for the Jackson Brownes, the Joni Mitchells, those types of writers that emerged. I think that was an incredible cycle, just like perhaps the Tchaikovskys and the Rimsky-Korsakovs and the Moussorgskys were at the end of the nineteenth century in Russia. I think that it was a cycle that we probably won't see again any time soon, unfortunately.

CG: *I hate to hear that. What was your family experience like as far as your personal training or support as you were growing up?*

DF: I was given obligatory piano lessons from ages six to ten or something, which I despised and tried to get out of in any way I could.

CG: *I did too.*

DF: I basically gave it up until my grandfather gave me a guitar when I was about eleven, and that's about . . . —eleven and twelve was the time the Beatles hit over here. That was what really made me want to get into it. I think you'll hear that from most people my age, that the Beatles were the real catalyst. I started studying guitar and played that in bands and rock bands until I was about fifteen or sixteen. Then I quit and became a solo act. When I went to college, I was just playing folk music and writing a lot of my own stuff by then. That was basically it. My father was a trained professional musician, as was my mother, so I always had music around the house when I was young.

CG: *What did they do?*

DF: My father was a bandleader and a player. He ran the Army Band during the war, out of Detroit—USO tours. Then he played in radio orchestras in Chicago. He played in speakeasies, jazz gigs, he played it all his life.

CG: *His instrument was what?*

DF: Many instruments. His classical instrument was oboe and his jazz instrument was sax—the tenor sax. But he was a conductor in later life and an educator and became the director of the music school at several universities and high schools.

CG: *And your mom?*

DF: My mother had a degree in classical voice from Bradley University in Illinois. She decided to have kids and become a mom instead of pursuing that, but she still can sing her head off.

CG: *If you had an opportunity to look at this interview as a portion of a book which students will read, what would you like to tell them as far as either how to develop their craft or how to think, philosophically?*

DF: Philosophically, I think the most important thing is that if you're really going to be a real artist and a real songwriter and devote your life to this, you can't be limited by the conventions of the music industry. The ones that have really made it the biggest and the best are the ones who battered down the doors of convention and lived their own way and didn't compromise too much. I think that it's very, very difficult and the odds are very (much) against you, but if there's a real artist out there who's writing music for purposes other than just making money and becoming famous or having a career in commercial music, then you've got to batter down the doors of conventionality. All the great ones have.

CG: *We're talking about the connection between art again.*

DF: Yeah, instead of toeing the line and doing what they want, you've got to make them come back after you. You've got to do something that isn't there before, that's unique, that really has a personality to it. Any slob can go ahead and write a hit song and have it for five years, but to maintain it over thirty, forty years is very difficult as a creative artist. The only way that I can see that you can do that is to be true to yourself and be true to your artistic instincts.

CG: *Do you have a particular work that you're most proud of or hang your hat on?*

DF: No, I sure don't. Every one is like a new child. The one I'm working on now is the most important one. I really don't much care about the past; that was then—this is now. The song I'm going to write tomorrow is the most important one.

CG: *Has your approach grown or changed over time—the craft?*

DF: Not markedly. I think I've matured. I think I'm a better artist, obviously. No, my approach has always been to wait for inspiration. I can't really force songs. I don't sit down and say, "Ok, I've got to write a song," and come up with something. It's generally composed out of waiting for inspiration and that can be a frustrating type of experience. I'm not as anxious as I used to be about it. I don't worry so much about the fact that I might go to the well the next time and have nothing there; I used to when I was young. Now, I feel very comfortable about it; this is why I'm meant to be here and my craft will be there when I need it. Whether it will be appreciated as much as it has (been) during different periods of my life, I have no idea and I really couldn't care less.

CG: *Right now, what disturbs me, is there seems to be a shift toward not only production of the recording, but a production of the performance as well. Do you approach performing your own music differently than writing it?*

DF: Do you mean on stage?

CG: *Yes.*

DF: No, I still believe in a live band, kicking. I may use a lot of machines on the record, but when I get on stage, I try to pare it down so musicians can actually play it. I don't believe that people should actually have to pay money to watch somebody lip sync and dance around. I'm out there to perform. That, to me, is as important as the original performance because that changes every night and it's a little bit dangerous and exciting.

CG: *With the video element, people want to go see what they just saw on their television set for free.*

DF: I don't know why. I always try to give something a different approach, twist it a little bit to make it interesting. Because I don't want to go out and see somebody play their record just like it was.

CG: *Since it is a world market now, and considering what we were discussing about record companies' attitudes in this country, is that the same worldwide? Are there pockets for creativity and different audience expectations elsewhere?*

DF: I think basically overseas is a less confining market, from what I've heard from people that go over there and play. There's more room for an artistic type of artist, especially in Europe, I think. There are people in this country that "can't get arrested" and over in Europe they sell quite a few records and do concerts. But, at the same time, Europe also loves country music. I don't know, I really haven't explored that much. People say to me, "Why don't you go play in France and all these places? They'd love you over there." And I say, "I just never have." I'm always so busy here that I've never found the time to do that.

Interview
with
Doug Wilde

Doug Wilde, an owner in the Canadian advertising agency Harris, Cole, Wilde, is one of Canada's premiere composers for the advertising industry and for film. His diversity as a jazz pianist, arranger,

211

composer and producer make him a creative powerhouse that is constantly in demand.

Mr. Wilde has been the musically creative force behind much of Canada's best advertisements for clients in Canada and the world markets. In fact, he has written over 1500 advertising scores for such clients as Diet Coke, Air Canada, Molson Breweries, and General Motors.

He won an International Hugo Award in 1989 for his score for the T.V. documentary, *The World Is Watching.* He also wrote the theme music for the CBC radio program *Sunday Morning.*

Mr. Wilde has made one recording, *Corsica,* which has not been released commercially.

CG

DW

CG: *Let's talk about your work. Do you work with storyboards from ad agencies and have a lot of content decisions made for you already?*

DW: It will happen in different ways. Sometimes the first thing we see will be a finished picture and at other times the first thing we see will be a storyboard. In either case, our job is to match the picture. If it's a storyboard, often what will happen is we'll do the music first and the editor will cut to what we do.

CG: *And you'll have some flexibility in the timings of it.*

DW: Yeah.

CG: *Do you ever start music first and they'll cut picture to it?*

DW: Quite a bit! Actually, that happens a lot more often.

CG: *So that's what happens most? Really?*

DW: Probably 40 to 50 percent of the time it happens that way.

CG: *How much of your business is divided up into national and international ads, regional ads, and local ads?*

DW: Well, almost everything we do is national and the odd thing is international. Very little is regional. Something to keep in mind though, in terms of Canada, the market is quite a bit different here because you have one country that's the size of the population base of New York State or California. So it's quite a bit different. To say something is national in the States is a larger market.

CG: *Have you done any analysis as to how the business is different in the States versus Canada? Or is it just geography and that's all?*

DW: No. No, I think there's a really big difference in how it's done in Canada, because it's a smaller country—not only in music, but in all of the production-and-supply creative areas. There's a lot more versatility in my opinion because you have to be versatile to survive. Whereas in the States, there would be companies that would specialize in doing synth scores or specialize in writing songs, or specialize in orchestral pieces, or specialize in radio production, or specialize in developing scripts and that sort of thing. In this country, you have to do all of those kinds of things well. That's one nice thing about it from my point of view is you get to work on all kinds of different projects and develop your skills at those.

CG: *International companies come to your agency for your country as opposed to shipping it in?*

DW: Usually, if we're doing something that is international, it will be through an advertising agency here that is producing something that they're going to be using throughout their international network of agencies. So if it's a big advertising agency, like J. Walter Thompson or someone like that, an agency that has a worldwide agency network, they might produce something here and find it's doing very well, and they might use it in a number of markets. For instance, we have one spot that's running all over the world now, and every few months we'll get a renewal. We'll get a check from places like Finland, Saudi Arabia, or Indonesia.

CG: *So you are in a creative market for a company worldwide then, not just the Canadian market?*

DW: Yeah, but that's pretty rare.

CG: *But GM and Coke come to you to do the Canadian versions, though, don't they?*

DW: Yeah, I see what you mean. We work on international products but those are all Canadian versions of those commercials. There are all sorts of creative concepts that are developed in this country and they would usually be different than what's done in the States.

CG: *So they have marketing strategies for every country and they handle it in the national agency?*

DW: That's right!

CG: *And if it happens to go over well and it's a uniform concept, then they may reuse it somewhere else?*

DW: It's fairly rare that that would happen, but sometimes it does happen.

CG: *I noticed on the demo reel that not everything fell into the standard edit spots, like :60 or :30 or :05; you had one thing for Air Canada that was over a minute.*

DW: That was something that's called the director's cut, where the director who shot it did a longer version of it for his reel—and I use that on my reel. I wrote the music to match that as well as the one that went to air.

CG: *And its designed to edit.*

DW: Yeah.

CG: *What's air there? What are the standard edits there? Is it :60s and :30s and :15s?*

DW: Usually its :60 and :30 and :15.

CG: *Maybe :05?*

DW: No, none that I've worked on, although I'm sure that they happen.

CG: *You know, just a little ID hook at the end.*

DW: Yeah.

CG: *And that's standard for radio and television?*

DW: I don't think you'll see very many :15s on radio. Mostly it'll be :60s and :30s because it's a lot less expensive.

CG: *It's starting to change in the last several years. When I was busy in ad work there were certain forms to jingles and it changed according to what market you were in—a regional, national or local spot—and if you weren't working from film or storyboard, if you were working on just the jingle, we used to do something we'd call a donut. You'd have your hook somewhere preceded by a verse; you may even start with your hook. You'd have some verse and you'd hook again right before your :30 edit. Then you'd have about :20 to :22 of bed material for which dialogue or voice-over would go in, and then you'd have your hook at the end, or any of those combinations. They would edit it out of a :60, but you wrote it for the purpose of donut editing.*

DW: Right, they'd pull out and make spaces where they wanted to.

CG: *Yeah. What's going on now is a lot more concept with the music and the film together, where the music doesn't carry all of the weight, and it's a lot more scoring.*

DW: That's right.

CG: *. . . and a lot more song forms rather than what I used to call jingle forms. Is that true?*

DW: Yeah, well, there's probably a different kind of approach, too. When you're dealing with corporate and national campaigns, you're more apt to have something that's smoother. Your not going to, in the middle of a national Air Canada spot, have a voice-over that comes in and says, "Available this week, get your special ticket sales . . . ," you know. They're more after the creation of a mood and consumer identification of the product as being something desirable as opposed to making you instantly go out and try to purchase something. It's more to imprint a favorable impression.

CG: *Where the whole thing creates and everything has its weight of content.*

DW: Also, the TV thing is different than the radio. Obviously we do jingles as well, not an awful lot of them compared to scoring. Scoring is a lot more of what we do. One spot in twenty might be a jingle. In terms of radio, one in five might be a jingle. So it's not as high a priority as it used to be. It's not something they use to sell products as much as they did twenty years ago with, "You wonder where the yellow went" or Brillcream.

CG: *Alka Seltzer is just a classic, you know, "blop, blop, fizz, fizz . . ."*

DW: But, there are the elements that come along and often they're the things that have worked for a long time, and an advertiser is reluctant to give something powerful up 'cause there's a lot of identification that people have with a strong melody and a strong concept.

CG: *When you do a jingle, do you have a standard form or do you write it out of concept?*

DW: Usually there'll be a lyric script we're given and they'll say, "We need a :10 voice-over and out" at this point or somewhere in it we need a :10 voice-over and out and we need this line that we've created to be in there somewhere. So, it's a little bit more flexible.

CG: *Do you write it in the longer format and then plan to tape edit it down into the smaller pieces, or do you do the whole piece in the smaller time frames?*

DW: It's definitely done that way.

CG: *Which way?*

DW: In the way that you would record it with everything in . . .

CG: *And then tape edit?*

DW: Yeah, but I can't remember the last time I did a jingle like that. So it's not done that often anymore. That format just isn't used that much here, but I know it's being done.

CG: *It seems like they use it a lot when they're introducing a new tune. If McDonald's has a new campaign this year and they're wiping out the old tunes that they've used and they're gonna try and implant the new tune . . .*

DW: Like, the "Food, Folks, and Fun" thing . . .

CG: *. . . then they'll put the jingle format in for several months, and after they've saturated the market with the tune, they'll begin to score and use the hook tags at the end.*

DW: Yeah, but I'm sure that they wouldn't use the same piece of music that they did at the beginning; they would do a different arrangement of it.

CG: *Oh yeah, for different markets.*

DW: Yeah, for a big advertiser, like McDonald's, they would certainly try and do that. The McDonald's one is a good example. The jingle itself was written by a Chicago company. I'm not certain of the exact company, but the execution of it for the Canadian market was by Canadian companies. So, we would have a lead sheet that would have the tune and the Canadian advertising agency would say, "OK, we need this picture to be scored and we want the ending melody of this jingle to be in there and we want you to use some of the musical ideas from the jingle."

CG: *So they dictate what portions of it you will use, so you don't have to make those choices?*

DW: No. But sometimes you do. There's no hard-and-fast rules for it. From one job to the next the whole palette changes, and in one thing you might have complete musical freedom and in another thing you might have a very limited area to work in.

CG: *So they do provide you with a lead sheet. It's not up to you to transcribe. We used to do a lot of Disney and Holiday on Ice stuff and they were featuring Donald one year. You had to yank out all of the Donald tunes from all of the Donald cartoons. You really had to do some research. You had to transcribe it and then you had to put it in the commercial, tie in* When You Wish Upon A Star *and all of this kind of stuff in two-bar quotes. You really had to do some research.*

DW: Wow.

CG: *You've got to make your impact (on an audience) in sixty seconds maximum . . .*

DW: Yeah, usually thirty . . .

CG: *How do you go about making decisions on what is the most effective (approach) and how you're going to work? To me, that is the hardest and most difficult job you have.*

DW: It's true, but in a lot of cases, the visual would be in place already or at least an idea would be in place in storyboard that has some kind of feel and some kind of climax to it. So first of all, the direction that you're going to take it in has already been defined in terms of where it peaks, where it pays off, and the point you're building to and that kind of thing; the shape of what you're doing is already in place, I think. Then, as Mike Post said, it really is a matter of sitting with the film. If there's no music reference that's been established, then it's a matter of sitting with the cut that you have or even sitting, looking at the storyboard, and trying to get a feel for what kind of music is going to work, first of all, and what kind of pacing is going to bring these pictures together and knit them together and highlight the right spots. That's really where the fun starts to happen because there's a lot of possibilities. Strangely enough, the job is easiest when the client says, "We want it to sound like this . . ." Or sometimes, we'll get a picture that already has a piece of music against it, it might be like a pop song or something from a film, and even though that limits us, it makes the job a lot easier because you already have a rhythm that's been defined and the picture has been cut to that rhythm, and you have an attitude that's been defined. The danger of that kind of thing, of course, is that if other people, besides yourself and the editor, see this and get used to the music they've used, there's the danger of people liking that too much and getting used to it and wondering why they can't have that. There's always a comparison point of what you're doing to some great pop song or some great piece of film music that you're trying to replace and do better than. There is always a current song that everyone's grabbing and putting against things. For years when I started in this business, it was *Chariots of Fire*, so you go into a meeting and somebody would put on the piece of film they've cut, and somebody would say, "We've got to do this really neat piece of music we've found. I'm not sure if you've heard this before, but listen to this." And you hear (the theme to *Chariots of Fire*), guys running in slow motion and all of this crap, you know. It was a beautiful piece of music, but it was used to death—and now the current one is *The Mission*. We'll go into these meetings and people pull out this piece of music and say, "I don't know if you've heard this, but it's really great. Listen to how it works with this picture," and then our eyes roll up into our heads, you know.

CG: *Ha, ha, then you pull up Mission copy #1 from your file and put it . . .*

DW: That's sort of how it goes.

CG: *In your Amnesty International thing, that seems to have a lot of dead cues you've got to hit, like the jail door slamming shut and things like that. When you've got dead cues and visual cues that you've got to hit and probably overdub sound effects with, do you write music to fit that or do you ignore it? It seems like you put it in there on strong beats or cadence points or things like that, you wrote with it.*

DW: In that particular case they gave us the film or the finished picture and I wrote the music to the picture. Of course, they would have SMPTE striped on the tape, so I would be able to know anything I had to hit, I could write it in or work towards that beat. Also, it wasn't a rhythmic piece that I wrote, it was more of a textural score.

CG: *It had rhythm in it, the pace of the walking feet, but that was more of an effect, instead of being in the fabric of the piece.*

DW: That's right.

CG: *Let me give you a hypothetical visual storyboard and let me see what you're going to do with it.*

DW: OK.

CG: *In terms now of thinking specifically, compositionally.*

DW: OK.

CG: *Let's say we've got an ecological piece here, some kind of save-the-earth thing. I start out with a zoom-in completely on the ground that's got grass and roots, like tree roots that come out above the ground and go back down, and the whole epic of this thing is thirty seconds. What it does is gradually pull back from that root to where it eventually shows the trunk of the tree, to the treetop, then goes above the tree to the sky and you see the surrounding forest; then, it goes to the stratosphere and eventually pulls back 'til you see the whole planet out in space. There's no dialogue except right at the end, where there's a voice-over that says, "It's up to you." It's thirty seconds and there's no specific cut angles you've got to hit, it's all one smooth pullback. From that hypothetic, compositionally, what are you going to do?*

DW: OK.

CG: *Think in sections: harmonic language, rhythm, harmonic rhythm, melody and melodic structure; if you're going to use a melody, how you would structure it, what language or mode it will be in, what the rhythm of the piece may be, how you'll deal with that and then the mechanics of it and orchestration last. Let me put you on the spot here.*

DW: There are two ways. The first thing I would think of would be in terms of shape. How would you like to shape the sound, regardless of what the sound is going to be? Whether it would be best to take it from a minimal sound and have it build to a grand sound at the end, you feel the earth, or conversely start it with something big and as you get farther away and you eventually see the planet, it's been reduced to something very small. Either way has a lot of impact. Maybe because "It's up to you" is the message at the end of it . . .

CG: *Which is individual . . .*

DW: Ending small might have a bit more impact or ending quietly, so that might be a way to approach this. In terms of rhythm, I see this as being not very rhythmic, maybe a texture kind of piece that would have smoother chords and textures of sound.

CG: *So you're going to have an implied rhythm and not metered and all that . . . ?*

DW: Yeah, all atmospheric because there's not going to be any hard cuts. Ideally it would be nice to do it with one camera move from the piece of grass to the planet, one camera move like that. There would be interesting ways of doing it. You could also do something like this with no music at all, just sound effects. That would be a whole other thing.

CG: *That's a neat idea.*

DW: Harmonically, a commercial like this is very, very unusual because, first of all, it's rare that there would be so little voice-over; and second, to have a concept that's so simple and even. So in terms of building it harmonically, the same thing would come to mind as came to mind structurally. Do I want to start this off very consonant and end it in a dissonant way, or do I want to start dissonantly and end in a consonant way? There are ways it could be structured. It doesn't seem like there could be many changes through the piece in terms of accenting things or melodic elements that you'd want to do because it seems like the whole idea is accenting the pullback of the camera. It seems to me the way to do it is to end it as quietly as possible, to start it close up and large and end it small. Start it close up and consonant and end it far away and dissonant. By doing that you would be starting off on this piece of grass, assuming that you don't know what this commercial is about, so that the farther away you went, the more dissonant it became and the more of a problem you saw was happening because this planet is being clogged up and polluted. As you ended up far away, there'd be a small little dissonant sound or a much smaller sound from the beginning. That's how I think of it.

CG: *That implies you can solve that problem with a variety of material. You can do it in a mode, or a minor mode, or no mode at all and use just intervalic counterpoint . . .*

DW: Yeah . . .

CG: *. . . with clusters and that kind if thing. Or you can do it with sound effects or both.*

DW: Yeah, probably the way I would do it would be a combination of sound effects. First of all, this is the kind of thing you'd want to try a few different things on and see what worked best, you know. One way to try it would be to approach it as a sound scape. What would be very effective would be the closeup of the grass, if you had a collage of sounds. It could be like street sounds and city sounds, people yelling and crowds, all sort of swirling around, and as you pull back these sounds get smaller and smaller or you'd keep taking more of these sounds from this collage until on your final picture there would be one sound left.

CG: *Like wind . . .*

DW: Yeah, wind or dissonance or something like that. And that's the same kind of thing you could do with just music regardless of whether it was synths or real instruments. By starting it consonantly and gradually moving notes or sections of the harmonic content so that it gradually became thinner and more dissonant. I wouldn't hear it being major and minor just because it tends to editorialize.

CG: *. . . and lock you in.*

DW: Yeah, I probably would go with a consonant kind of fourths and fifths kind of sound, and as it got farther away bring in seconds and sevenths and ninths and move that way.

CG: *A visual implication that gives an underlying current to it is urgency. You don't know from the storyboard what speed the camera is moving, but let's say it increases in speed to the end, quick and to a halt.*

DW: Yeah, that would certainly make me try it a different way.

CG: *How would you deal with rhythm here?*

DW: If I knew it would start on a single picture and then gradually pick up speed, then suddenly stop, it would really be nice to have some kind of tribal rhythm that would pick up about the :10 point, and assuming that the pullback would increase in speed, start some type of rhythm there and adding to it in terms of levels. I'm thinking maybe a West African 12/8 pattern, something like that, that would have different levels. . .

CG: *. . . or subdivisions to it.*

DW: Yeah, so that you would hear first, dum, dum, dum, dum, and then dum ta da, dum ta da, and then you could hear dum tee dee, dum tee dee (in quarter-note triplets), all these different levels that would grow into it. Not necessarily using the ethnic instruments, but using this kind of thing that could really build an intensity, then suddenly stopping. That's another way this commercial would really work—just using percussion instruments starting at the :10 point with your pullback, maybe having a few little accents starting on your first shot and stopping on the planet.

CG: *I look at music as not just that which is vibration produced either acoustically, synthetically, or digitally, but the whole sound environment and its possibilities including sound effects. All of which have musical aspects like rhythm and timbre and color . . .*

DW: That's right.

CG: *Do you do a lot of planning compositionally and orchestrationally for sound effects or nonconventional devices?*

DW: Yeah, I certainly use it a lot in my work. Also, for each project I will have sounds that aren't musical sounds readily available that have been created for the job or come from a library of things that we have around that I know will work. For instance, that Diet Coke spot with the skater. In that one there's helicopter sound effects for him twirling that I had around from another job that weren't recognizable in the same way. I knew I wanted to find something interesting for his spinning, and the helicopter sound seemed to really work. It doesn't sound like a helicopter necessarily in the piece, it sounds like some kind of airy rhythm thing that's happening.

CG: *Was that done by some direct electronic manipulation of that sample or was it done in the mix?*

DW: A combination of both. So that kind of thing is used an awful lot.

CG: *What's your turnover time from when you get an assignment versus when it's out? What's normal for you?*

DW: Well, the range is amazing. Usually, a few days to a week. The longest I can think of is a year and the shortest I can think of is writing it in the recording studio. I have my machines sitting there, the client leaves the room for a half an hour, and I write the music in the studio.

CG: *That doesn't give you a whole lot of time to do anything complex.*

DW: No, but it does happen and some of the best stuff we've done has been done that way. Something has to get done right away—and there's a sales meeting at two the next day—and it's got to be done, and there's no choice about it.

CG: *Do they do the voice-overs first?*

DW: Often they're done first. There's really no rule for that. It really depends. If it's a read that's being scored for radio, they would often do the voices first because that's really your only reference point if you're going to score something. If it's for TV, it's more specific.

CG: *Do you have a great need to keep up with the neighbors as far as national competition, what's going on in the States, what's hot? What degree do you have to be concerned with current cliche?*

DW: First of all, we all listen to what's happening in pop and the film world an awful lot. Those reference points are used by us and the people we work for, too. So when they say, "We want Edie Brickell and the New Bohemians," or, "We want The Pet Shop Boys, or R.E.M. or something that sounds like that," we've got to know what that sounds like, or at least know enough about it to go and buy the record and listen to it. Or if the reference point is the sound of another commercial, we have to have access to that kind of thing and we certainly study. We're always ordering international reels from Europe or the States to see what other people are doing.

CG: *So there's a whole lot of ongoing research?*

DW: Yeah, it's really fun to see what people are doing. One thing about Canada is that the audio side of the business is very strong. There are several companies here that are very, very good. Most of the sound that's done for Canadian commercials is done and recorded and produced in Canada; whereas, a lot of the pictures are produced by Americans for our market. What I mean by that is they're made by Canadian agencies, but they'll use an American director or an American editor or American talent in the spot; but almost always the sound is done here. The odd times it will be done by a company in New York or London, but not that often.

CG: *What are your roots musically? How did you get to where you are? What did you listen to as a kid? What do you listen to now? What is your training? What shapes your whole language?*

DW: Coming from a musical family, and always having my mom playing show tunes on the piano and my dad playing old jazz tunes. It was always around the house. Like every kid of that era, really liking pop music and getting into the Beatles and all that in the early seventies. Discovering this new kind of jazz that was happening. Really sparking my interest by hearing Chick Corea and that sort of jazz thing, *Light As a Feather* and those kinds of albums. Suddenly getting interested in this stuff and wanting to study it. I learned to play guitar and piano by ear and in my late teens wanting to get more serious about it and learning how to read and taking a Berklee correspondence course around that time. I decided that I wanted to really study and I studied by myself to get my piano chops up and got into music school in Canada.

CG: *Where did you go?*

DW: I went to a school called Humber College and to the University of Western Ontario, to York University, and to Eastman.

CG: *You were at Eastman three years (the Arrangers Workshops in the summers)?*

DW: No, four.

CG: *Four. What did you take? We were together in the arrangings.*

DW: Arranging twice, film scoring, and the synth courses they had.

CG: *How was that for you?*

DW: I enjoyed that a lot. The focus of my previous studies was on being a good jazz player and writing for big bands. I started to turn off of that. I wanted to write for pictures and film, so I got to Eastman and got that stuff happening. I took some conducting courses here, and by the time something came available here, I had enough of my skills together. Also, synthesizers had been evolving through the late seventies and eighties. To work in this business, you have to have a really good understanding of this technology, so I was trying to keep up with that at the same time.

CG: *Do you provide that function for the company as far as you being the technology expert as well as creative, or does somebody else wear that hat?*

DW: No, no, I do both.

CG: *That's hard, isn't it?*

DW: Yeah, but it's also my company and I'm not going to say to myself, "You're not hip enough, you're not doing a good job, you're fired," you know. I mean there are limits, and when I'm in over my head, I'll get some help. But I've got a pretty good grip on all of the MIDI gear, samplers, computers, and keyboards.

CG: *What would you tell kids who have a lot of skill and a lot of dreams, and are basically young and their listening and playing experiences are limited, but they want to get into some aspect of the industry in either playing, songwriting, production, or advertising, or all of the above. What would you tell them as one who has paid some dues and become successful?*

DW: First, I would say, "Listen to as many types of music as you can possibly find, whether you like it or not." Second, I would say, "Listen in as many different ways as you can. What I mean by that is don't just listen to the music; listen to the production as well. Don't just listen to the song or melody; listen to the other things that are happening in the music. Listen to the rhythm. Listen to an orchestral piece and just listen to what the rhythm is doing—or listen to a jazz piece and think about what the background voices are doing, the background harmonies, how different voices are moving. Listen in terms of counterpoint. Listen in terms of rhythm, in terms of texture, in terms of orchestration. There are a lot of things to be learned by listening to one piece of music a hundred times. If it's a good piece of music, you can learn as much as listening to a hundred different pieces. In addition to that, write as many different kinds of music as you can and write them as many different ways as you can, if being a writer is what you want to do. If being a professional writer is what you want to do, then your job, at least in this end of the business, is to be able to write any kind of music and write it well."

CG: *And know where to dig it up, and find reference points and how to duplicate and all that.*

DW: That's right. That's right! Study harmony, study orchestration. I think that goes without saying, though. Those are the basic things that you have to know. There's no question that you've got to be able to sit down with a sheet of manuscript paper and write stuff out if you need to or that you have to sit in front of a computer and to know how to access the different MIDI channels and how to edit on the computer. These are all basic skills that are absolutely essential in this world now. As much as all of this, it's really important to develop your personal skills and social skills. It's a hard fact that a lot of people come to after spending years studying the mechanics and the art of music. You come into the real world and you realize that you're not getting any work or you're not successful. You might be the best writer in the world, but if you're not able to function well with other people, you won't make it. It's important because you're working in a service industry and you've got to be able to service your clients and give them what they want with a smile and make them feel really comfortable. That's something that a lot of hermit musicians like myself have had a hard time dealing with. It's really hard when you have to be a businessman after years of trying to be an artist.

CG: *Now how does that function day to day with you? Do you have a percentage of work that you're just not happy with because it wasn't artistic in scope, but it did fill the prescription and they're happy with it and they've paid their bill and I can now eat this week? Or do you have enough control to where you really are pleased with it?*

DW: We have a fair bit of control. I'm almost always happy with what goes out of the door. Although it is painful, when for reasons you can't control, an exceptional piece of work becomes just good . . . but that's part of the job. I think its really important to have your skills together. Artistic satisfaction is a whole other thing. One part of it is doing your job well and giving your client what they want, and the other side of that is feeling really good about what you've given them. Ideally, you want both sides to be a plus, and I think most of the time we're able to do that. I feel good about it.

CG: *Speaking strictly entrepreneurally, because every working musician has to have some business skills, do you have any advice on how to get work and keep work?*

DW: (It's) important for people to know who you are. When you're creating music for advertising, it's often a company, as opposed to an individual, that approaches the industry. It's a lot more difficult for me to get on the phone and call up a hundred agencies and a hundred different producers and say, "Can I come in and present my reel to you?" It's very hard for one person to take care of all of that and still be writing music. But, when you're starting out, it's often that way. You've got to be able to present yourself and do the research needed to find out who people are and how willing they are to hear what you have to offer. We're in a good position because we've established our client base; we don't have to go out and knock on doors to get work. However, I also write outside of the advertising business for films and for documentaries. That's work that I have to hunt down myself and keep happening. The difficult thing about that world, for me, is that it's a whole different group of people. It's a group of people that don't produce thirty spots a year. They might produce a few films every year or two. And even if you have a good contact in that business, a person who likes you a lot and wants to use you, there's no reason why they're going to use you for everything they do. They may want different attitudes or different kinds of results from the music. It's really a hard world for someone not terribly aggressive businesswise to break into.

CG: *There are no companies for that, are there!*

DW: When you see a film it's not often you'll see "Music Produced by: Best Music Inc." It's almost always an individual's name you will see.

CG: *Aren't there agents for that, though!*

DW: Yeah, there are film agents in L.A. Its not that big a market up here though, it's a different kind of thing. Do you have Ray Wright's book?

CG: On the Track! *Yeah, it's right here in front of me.*

DW: Great book!

CG: *Yeah!*

DW: In there he talks about how writing for commercial advertising is thought of as an apprenticeship for writing for film. It really is because you're using all the same skills. In a sense you're working a lot more intensely, and it's great training.

CG: *It seems like it's almost a relief when you get a film because you've got more time to deal with. You're just dealing in gestures in advertising, but they have to be the right ones and that's a skill in itself.*

DW: For me, I feel if I want to go further along the compositional lines in that market, it's really a matter of making contacts in the States because that business doesn't really exist on a large scale here.

CG: *What about Europe! Is that an easier jump for you than the States!*

DW: It would be just as hard. There are more people who go from Toronto to L.A. than from Toronto to London.

CG: *Do you have a lot of international competition into this kind of thing! Is Japan making progress or is it still a North American entity!*

DW: For . . . ?

CG: *For commercials and film, for what we do.*

DW: I've never seen any spot produced by a Japanese company for a Canadian advertiser.

CG: *I had a line on a B-movie company to do all their work, real assembly-line stuff. They were out of California, but he got it cheaper in Hong Kong.*

DW: I'm sure that kind of thing happens.

CG: *Is there anything that I haven't asked you that we need to talk about?*

DW: Well, it is an awful lot of fun. I feel fortunate to be making a living doing something that I love to do. There are a lot of things I've talked about already, the technology, writing for different-size ensembles, creating unique sonic environments, and doing it all quickly. There's a sign that we like to put on our door. It says, "Quick, Good, Cheap, Pick Any Two." Most people that come to us would like all three. More often than not, it's good and fast.

Interview
with
Mike Post

Mike Post has had an enormously successful twenty-year career as a musician, composer, arranger, and producer. He has toured the Los Angeles club circuit, appearing with a variety of acts, and has played for such famous artists as Sammy Davis, Jr. and Sonny and Cher. He became the youngest musician in history to hold the position of musical director of a television show, when at twenty-four he held that position for "The Andy Williams Show." He also produced shows for televion including "The Mac Davis Show."

Post's most visible accomplishments have been composing music for television and film. His credits include:

"L.A. Law," "Hooperman," "Wiseguy," "The Phil Donahue Show," "Hunter," "Doogie Howser, M.D.," "Law & Order," "Quantum Leap," "Cop Rock," "The Rockford Files," "The Greatest American Hero," "The A-Team," "The White Shadow," "Riptide," "Hardcastle & McCormick," "Hill Street Blues," "Sonny Spoon," "The Joan Rivers Show," "Toma," "Baa Baa Black Sheep," and "Magnum P.I."

In addition to scoring, Post continues to work as a record producer and arranger. He is the winner of five Grammy awards and has produced recordings for Polydor/Polygram and other labels. Among these recordings are his own *Music from "L.A. Law" & Otherwise* and *The Theme from "Hill Street Blues,"* and in conjunction with Stephen Geyer, *The Theme from "The Greatest American Hero"*; also, *The First Edition*, featuring Kenny Rogers, *I Just Dropped In (to See What Condition My Condition Was In)*, Mason Williams' *The Mason Williams Phonograph Album*, which includes the hit, "Classical Gas," Dolly Parton's *Nine To Five*, and Peter Allen's, *I Could've Been a Sailor*.

CG

MP

CG: *What is your activity in Los Angeles as a composer? Is it all television music?*

MP: Yeah, it's 90 percent TV.

CG: *How many pilot projects and things do you work on?*

MP: Well, I'm doing four pilots this pilot season and I currently have "Doogie," "Law and Order," "L.A. Law," that I'm doing the music for this season, and then a new show that sold for 13 called "Blackjack Savage"—that's four. So I'm working on four shows as a composer myself, and I'm packaging three more that other composers are doing for my company, and I've got four pilots.

CG: *Is a pilot just the one episode or a series?*

MP: The one.

CG: *When you're previewing something, what decisions do you make?*

MP: Well, the first thing that happens, as you may or may not know, the composer is the last guy in, so I get a finished product, except it doesn't have any music on it. Most composers have to go to the studio where the film is made and sit down with the associate producer or the line producer, who are usually the ones in charge of overseeing the composer's duties. At this point in my career, I don't do that. Basically, what I do is the film gets sent to me on videotape and I spot the picture by myself, without somebody from the production company. I decide where the music's going to stop and start, so that's the first decision—where the music goes. Then I make a list of those cues the music editor does, and I fax them back to the producer. The executive producer is the guy I usually work with, so I don't even mess with the line producer or the associate producer. I fax it back to him and sometimes, as in the case of "L.A. Law," I discuss it with the executive producer as to what I'm going to do and how I'm going to do it, get his thoughts on it, and then after that, a day or so, I get the breakdowns from my music editor of those scenes that I've decided to play, and I start from there.

CG: *Is it customary that whoever is doing the music score do the opening title and closing credits and all scene changes as well, or is that farmed out to somebody else due to your status in the city?*

MP: What usually happens here is somebody gets hired to do a pilot, and in doing that pilot, he does the main title and he does all the score as well. Now whether he stays with the show or not is usually up to the production company, and depending on his schedule, whether he's a TV guy or a film guy and he's on to a movie or something like that. In my particular case I've never created and abandoned. I've stayed with the shows that I do from the beginning and I don't farm anything out until I'm ready to give the show lock, stock, and barrel to someone else, as in the case of "Quantum Leap" in the second year, as in the case of "Hunter" in the fifth year, as in the case of various other shows that I've done where my schedule has gotten so tight and the show is so demanding and on such a tight schedule that I've gone on and hired another composer to do the subsequent scores. Obviously, the main title stays the same. The main title stays mine, but the score each week will be done by another composer.

CG: *Are there formats that are like production-generated bylaws of how long a title is going to be, how long credits are going to be, what are in-and-outs?*

MP: Yes. There's no format in terms of score, no.

CG: *I mean in timings and lengths.*

MP: No, no. There's no format in terms of scoring in-and-outs. That's what I think you mean by scoring, don't you?

CG: *Well, main titles too, both. In-and-outs, main titles, credits too.*

MP: In the case of hour drama, there is no formula for the score, and the score consists of play-ons, play-offs, and the music under the drama, sometimes called stings or this and that; but in my language it's just score. The main title and the end credits, there is somewhat of a format for that. In half-hour sitcoms, they're always one minute, except that ABC requests a 30-second main title and a 45-second main title, but basically it's a one-minute main title; but in hour drama you have between a minute and a minute, 20 seconds, usually, to make a main title.

CG: *Is that your decision or a producer's decision?*

MP: Well, it's both.

CG: *Since you receive a finished product, is that already decided for you to just fill the hole in, then?*

MP: No. Because, when I say I'm the last guy in, in a pilot situation, the main title is not shot until the music is completed 'cause they cut the main title to the music. So usually, I come up with a piece of music and if it's a minute and 10 seconds long or a minute and 15 seconds long, that doesn't really matter—they'll adjust to me.

CG: *So titles are submitted, then, on an audition basis, is that an assumption that's accurate, people shopping different titles as possibilities?*

MP: Not in my case. I don't ever audition.

CG: *With your status, I guess not.*

MP: I don't. I audition in the respect that, "Hey, listen, I've come up with a piece of music, how do you guys like it," you know, and if they don't like it I'll come up with another one.

CG: *Do they give you general guidelines?*

MP: Well, of course. (a) I'm going to read a script. (b) I may even see some "dailies" or some early piece of film, but you know I will definitely take their (advice). We'll sit down and say, "Well, what kind of piece of music do you think?" For sure, I want to get the guy who created the show's feel because that's the guy I'm working for and I've got to please him.

CG: *When you're looking at a piece of film and making decisions either for title or scores and you're looking at a blank piece of score page—the writer's horror, having to look at a blank piece of score paper—to what degree do you make an intellectual choice versus an instinctual choice of things like harmonic language? What mode you'll be in, if any? What melodic structure? If you could just take me through your process?*

MP: All those are instinctual and they're different for the score than they are for the main title. A main title, as I said, you don't have a piece of film to look at, they're going to cut to you. I'm going to sit down with the guys and say, "What's going to start this *Hill Street Blues* off?" "Well, we were thinking of a car coming out of a precinct house and driving through a bunch of burned-out, bombed-down, mean streets, rain coming down, snow coming down, OK, OK."

CG: *So it's very similar to working with a storyboard on a jingle?*

MP: Well, somewhat, except you don't have the specificity that you do in a jingle, but you know they've described a picture to you. In doing the score you're looking at a piece of picture and you say, "How do I want to manipulate the audience? How do I want to support this piece of drama or action?" So, it's more intellectual when you're talking about score, and it's more instinctual when you're talking about main title. And I can run you through the order in which I ask myself the questions I ask myself.

CG: *OK.*

MP: The first question I ask is, "What kind of music is this, happy, sad, action, sexy?"—you know, those kinds of questions. Well, in the terms of score, you're looking right at it, so what's on the screen is going to tell you what kind of music it is. The next big giant question is, "What tempo is it?" And you don't even think about that, you just start tapping your foot. I mean you just go, "Ah hell, I know what this is."

CG: *What do you look at to derive the tempo? The speed of scene changes?*

MP: The speed of the cuts, the speed of how the camera's moving, how the action that's being photographed is moving.

CG: *So it's very obvious to you?*

MP: Yeah, extremely obvious. Now, within the framework of it being obvious, you can obviously go against it. *Hill Street* goes against what a cop show ought to open up like, especially one that's so "streety" and mean and funky. That should have opened up, you know . . .

CG: *. . . screaming.*

MP: Yeah. B. B. should have opened that show.

CG: *Is that a deliberate choice on your part?*

MP: Yeah, hell yeah. Meant to do it and they meant for me to do it 'cause we discussed it. Bochco and I sat down and he said, "Well, what would you normally do." And I said, "Well, something really streety and funky, burned-out neighborhood. Hell yeah, it'd be, you know, black and funky." He said, "Well, what else?" I said, "Well, you could go completely against it and kind of try something poignant, you know, that just makes you shake your head. Yeah, you could do something different." He said, "Yeah, do that," and that's all that was said. I went home and wrote that. So it differs from when you're writing a piece of score where it's right there in your face, it's right on the screen in front of you, and you know right away what you've got to do 'cause the tempo is set, the kind of music is set by what's being photographed, what's being said. Then the next decision you make is, you go, "OK, what is the sound of this scene?" Well, you know, and that's a process of orchestration, you go, "Well, gee, it's kind of a string thing, I think here. OK, I know what the tempo is, but I could treat it in the woodwinds or I could treat it in the strings or I could treat it in the rhythm section—nah, nah, this is a string thing—yeah, the texture of it should be the strings." Then you start to get specific . . .

CG: *. . . as to how, how you're going to pull it off?*

MP: Well, that's easy. The how's easy, because if there's a definite tempo to the thing you know it's going to click, OK. If you don't want people pattin' their feet to it, if you want it to go gently and you want it to move around tempowise, then you're definitely doing it to picture. In which case you use the Newman method, streamer and punches, and you conduct it. It's that simple. Of course, the rule of thumb for me, I would never not use a click if it was any faster than three seconds a bar, OK.

CG: *Right.*

MP: So if it's slower, if it's three seconds a bar or slower and you're never going to go any slower than six seconds a bar of four, that's the slowest you'll ever want to be. Usually, even in the slowest scenes you'll want to be around five seconds a bar. Then your how is really easy to do 'cause you just sit down with your cue sheet and you say, "OK . . . , here's a one-minute, 15-second scene." Basically the thing that sets us apart from the Ernest Golds of yesteryear or the Alfred Newmans of yesteryear, is that we're all following in (Henry) Mancini's footsteps, in that we want to write tunes, basically. So that dictates that you don't catch everything, that you don't change the music every time the camera cuts, you don't change the music every time somebody sneezes or every time a bird flies across the screen. You make a piece of music to go from, well, "Let's see, I can go from 00.00, I can go all the way to :34 before I've got to catch anything or impact anything. OK, so I'll make a little tune from there to there. OK, I've got to make a shift at :37.6; you underline that." OK. You look that up in your click track book, or in the case of a freetiming thing, you make your bars come out so that that becomes a downbeat or a third beat or something that you can hit and catch with a streamer. And then, you know, you basically find those two or three little points in that 1:15 that you want to point up musically and you design your music to do just that. It's that simple. And in the meantime, you don't pay attention to timings, you don't pay attention to the fact that you had to accommodate a picture. You write a piece of music that plays that much of the picture in your heart.

CG: *To what degree are you limited by budget in terms of concepts and orchestration choices?*

MP: Tremendously, I mean you have a budget and you must work within it.

CG: *Do you orchestrate all of your own material?*

MP: Yes.

CG: *Is that standard?*

MP: Yeah. In television I'd say that most guys orchestrate their own stuff.

CG: *Is your stuff mostly live or sequenced?*

MP: About half and half now. Not within a show, in other words, I mean, I have shows that are sequenced, but I do a show either live or sequenced. Basically, "L.A Law" is live, "Doogie" is live in that it's just a little Rhodes and some synth strings, but I play them live. I do that different than any other show because I don't write it, I play it. I look at the picture and play it. "Law and Order" I sequence, but I write it, and then it's sequenced.

CG: *To what degree do the session players create what's happening when you do a live thing? In the case of "Hill Street," is the exact voicing written . . .*

MP: Yep . . .

CG: *. . . or is what is published a transcription?*

MP: Nope. I wrote exactly what I wanted played out of the piano.

CG: *The whole thing?*

MP: Yeah, of course, darn right. But, in the guitar part I wrote "Fill," I wrote E flat and I wrote "Fill," and then Larry Carlton played a fill, and it's that simple. In the drum part I'll write the first couple of bars and then draw a line. The bass part I write specifically, and in the drum part when I want something specific, I write it.

CG: *Who makes the decision on titles as to whether it's going to be instrumental or vocal?*

MP: The producer and myself.

CG: *Do you do lyrics yourself?*

MP: No, "The Greatest American Hero," the biggest hit I've been involved in that's had lyrics, is written by Steven Geyer, and it was fun to do that. We've done a couple of others together. We've got one on the air called "Blossom," a sitcom, and Dr. John sang the main title for us.

CG: *You go in with the full vocal score and they're reading it, instead of creating during the session!*

MP: Definitely.

CG: *I'm trying to get a handle on your particular impression of what drives your sound harmonically. Do you perceive yourself as having a style . . .*

MP: Yes.

CG: *. . . that is unique from other people and helps attract business to you!*

MP: No. I don't know how unique it is to other people, my style in terms of "modus operandi" on an intellectual level. Nobody has done anything new since Mancini, and we're all following his particular path in how to score film, in that before him, it was all classical guys that changed the music at every drop of the hat. Then Hank came in and said, "Let's send these people out hummin' these things and let's write tunes, and weave those tunes with our orchestration ability and our picture sense to cover the drama and then only when applicable, let's write pure score that isn't a tune. Let's go ahead and be very orchestral with it, very nonmelodic, but basically, let's try and look for a melody"—and I follow that strictly. The thing that may make me a little bit different from some of the other guys is that I was a rock-and-roller that learned to read, write, orchestrate, and conduct, as opposed to a classical kid or a jazz kid that learned something about contemporary music. When my partner Pete Carpenter and I first did "Rockford Files" nobody did television with guitars. I mean it just wasn't done. Nobody had ever heard of a dobro and nobody had ever heard of a volume pedal against a sort of a fourth chord in the strings going "eeeooww, eeeooww," to be spooky. Nobody had ever used those rock-and-roll tricks, and we knew 'em. When I brought my mini moog onto stage 10 at Universal to go, "bee-amp, bow, bee-dee-amp, bow," nobody had ever seen a mini moog. They didn't know what the f--- I was talking about. So, because they were all jazz guys and classical guys, they didn't know a fuzz tone from anything. It's just that I was the first rock-and-roller to walk in the door in those days. It was us and them, all of you guys in school and all us guys on the street. I was the first one that knew how to read, or how to orchestrate or conduct, or that knew language. So that was my little ticket on this bus, and if I've been able to do anything different, it's because I have a different sort of a background. I basically skipped jazz. I played rock-and-roll music and listened to a ton of classical music and studied a ton of classical music. But, I also studied rock-and-roll music and the roots of it, blues, in the most disciplined way that I could. It wasn't being taught in school, but I think of myself as a pretty good musicologist in the roots of rock-and-roll. I think that's helped me a great deal. I think it's helped me sound a lot different from the guys that were rolling out of Eastman having really torn Stravinsky apart, having really torn Hindemith apart, really being extremely accomplished serial writers. When they hit town they'd say, "Well, let me write some score."

CG: *How do you think that applies conceptually—a neoclassic view in training versus a jazz point of view in training versus a rock-and-roll point of view—as far as the approach?*

MP: I think my background makes it possible to write more accessible melodies that people are going to walk out hummin'. It's just that simple.

CG: *Have you ever had a need to justify that in your career? Have you fought any battles in your career because of that?*

MP: No, sure haven't. But, I know that that gets talked about once in a while, but it doesn't get talked about to me. Basically, my friends hire me and they like what I write, and then every once in a while the public goes out and buys a million of it, and it feeds my wife and kids.

CG: *That's all the validation you need.*

MP: I wasn't trying to do anything else. I wasn't trying to do anything more than to write a piece of music that somebody liked and that I liked.

CG: *You keep talking about melody, and I think that is the prime factor in scoring, which may be really subtle and most people pass over when they're just viewing a piece. How do you approach melodic creation, which may be the most nebulous of all things and very much centered in your roots and how it filters through your intuition, through your training and experiences?*

MP: That's true, it's exactly right. It is centered, exactly. I look at film without music and start hummin'.

CG: *And you transcribe your hum in essence?*

MP: It just happens to me.

CG: *Has it always been that way or has there been a time when you had to mechanically make something work?*

MP: No, every single time. That's a button I push and it's automatic. Now it isn't always the thing, they don't always like it, and I don't always like it a day later or something—but s---, I'm never out of ideas. I look at something and I go, "Ah, I know what that ought to be." You know it's just easy for me, and that's the definition of a guy in the perfect job. If I was in a conservatory and (you) told me that I was going to have to come up with some, you know, some new idea on how to massage a row, it might not be easy for me. I'm just the perfect guy in the perfect job, I think.

CG: *Most people, myself included, when I try to write a commercial thing, I have an idea and I transcribe my idea and let it go where it wants to go, and try to make it fit a structure that is coherent and has some flow to it. The next thing, for me, is to do the lead sheet and changes for it and make them as accommodating to it as possible. But the most scary thing, as an arranger, is the scoring part of it, when you're deciding to dictate the bass part, as you said, or the piano part, if necessary, the exact voicings, or to leave it up to the player. The most intrinsic thing that most people have difficulty with is the groove, what to label the groove. How does a groove specifically mold each individual tune, because everything, whether considered rock ballad, pop, samba, etc., as a generic category, will eventually get a cohesion around the melody. Is there a trick in helping make that work or is that left to chance with the players?*

MP: Absolutely not.

CG: *How do you approach groove?*

MP: See, that's where my background serves me very well.

CG: *You're a pianist?*

MP: A guitar player and pianist, and it's so simple. To me, groove was first in my life, so it's the first thing I ever learned, not the last thing. I took "Groove 1" before I took harmony. I took "Groove 1" before I took dictation or melody or orchestration or any of that. I mean the first time I ever heard Robert Johnson or Chuck Berry or any of that, it was, you know . . . The first time I ever heard Ray Charles and copped a lick, it was "Groove 1." The first time I ever realized that all that "da deet dee da-doo-lee-op da deep dee," that that lick was Professor Long Hair and not Ray Charles, I was getting my groove lessons. What I do is I rely on my ability to write very specifically, combined with my ability to hire the right guys, combined with my ability to speak English and to refer back to other . . .

CG: *Similar. . .*

MP: . . .Yeah, to make similes, with these guys, to make analogies that, "Nah, nah guys, don't you remember, it's like this, like that Philadelphia thing." And because I can play two of the instruments, three of the instruments, because I'm also a bass player, I can play three of the instruments in a rhythm section pretty well and I can write drums and percussion as well as anybody can write it, then, it's not a problem for me to get my groove across. It's just not a problem. I'm not a violin player that has learned what a guitar is, I'm a guitar player who's learned what a violin is. And so if you ask me to take the Penderecki *Violin Concerto* and make a piece that was analogous to that, I'd have my hands full, I'd really have to work hard.

CG: *To what degree do you have to edit? When you get the caliber of players that you work with, and you're in a session and it begins to happen like it's supposed to happen, it may take on a life of its own. Is there a good deal of editing where you say, "Wait a minute, this is hip; but this is not going to work for prime time?"*

MP: Not really. These guys are so "pro" and I have so much communication built up over 22 and 23 years, you know, that I don't have to ride herd on 'em much. And you also have to understand, it's one of those kinds of deals where the guys are old friends of mine and we've hung out a lot together; so because of that, it's sort of short handed. Everything can be dealt with without a big deal. You also have to understand one thing, anybody, even the most specific guys, and I'm really, for a rock-and-roller, I'm extremely specific as a writer. But the magic of music is I know how it's gonna sound, you know how it's gonna sound, hell, we've done this for so many years, but you still go in there and you still drop a downbeat and you go, "Well g...... it, I knew it was gonna sound that way, but I didn't know it was gonna sound THAT WAY." And you're surprised by it and you're intrigued by it and you're made happy by it. Now it used to be in the old days, I can remember sessions I did in the old days like *Classical Gas* and things like that where I was so, I was so nervous and so unsure of myself that, man, I was specific about every little drop of everything. Man, I overwrote that down to bow markings, down to, you know, stupid stuff that when you have really good professional studio musicians and you're going to be there and conducting, it's ridiculous to write all that garbage. It's just overkill. It's just more s... for them to look at on the page and confuse them, rather than let them play the music. So, I really have found that maybe it's 80 percent—20 percent nowadays. Even if you're terribly specific, you're still 20 percent those guys, their hearts are gonna be showin' through that music. It's a collaborative effort.

CG: *What type of things do you do for yourself now, or is it all business?*

MP: I hum a lot and I listen a tremendous amount.

CG: *What do you like to listen to? What are your influences now?*

MP: Well, I still listen to a lot of Dvorak.

CG: *Why? What do you get out of his music?*

MP: Well, this is a guy who took folk melodies, he took music of the people and made wonderful symphonies. I still listen to Shostakovitch a lot.

CG: *I like him for rhythm.*

MP: Me too.

CG: *He's very rhythmic and logical.*

MP: It's very followable. I still listen to the blues a lot. I listen to ethnic music a tremendous amount. I've been hung up on Irish music for ten years.

CG: *Is that for research purposes?*

MP: No, just for enjoyment purposes. And I love, you know, if you hear a really crack Irish band, what they do is they play the same melodic passages over and over and just add more ornamentation. And I'm fascinated by the ornamentation in Eastern European music, like that Bulgarian women's choir, you ever heard that thing?

CG: *Yeah.*

MP: Just savage music. I've been listening to some Bulgarian music just for the embellishment, it's just so, wow, fierce. And it's right next door to the Irish music. The Irish music is extremely fierce. So I've always been a kind of folky collector of all these weird things.

CG: *Have you ever found the necessity to do ethnic research for the purpose of commercial application, or do you do what you do and they come to you for what you do, and what you see is what you get? Or, I'm not going to do country one day and I'm not going to do blues one day and I'm not going to do Shostakovitch one day, or do people have to do that when you're establishing a career?*

MP: Sure you have to do it because they bring you pictures that speak to subjects that are covered by different kinds of music—so you have to be able to say, "Gee, somebody remade *Les Miserables*. I gotta find out about eighteenth-century French music." There's no ifs, ands, or buts about it. Now it's all filtered through your creativity . . .

CG: *A lot more documentaries get off into the ethnic origins, rather than prime time.*

MP: Plus, it gives you more ammo, you know. The more you hear, the bigger your ears are and the smaller your ego is, the better composer you're gonna be. I mean, let's admit it. Listen, since Bach died, this is all a big D.C. anyway, so . . .

CG: *Ha, ha, that's right.*

MP: It's not like you or I are gonna come up with anything different. There's twelve of those f_____ and one of them is an octave. This is finite. We're not looking into black holes and wondering what's out there. People don't realize that, but you and I do, and everybody with a brain in their a__ is gonna say, "Hey, you know something, a triad's a triad." What you can hope to do is to come up with some colors or combinations that haven't been tried yet in exactly the same way—and that's a whole lot of fun.

CG: *Do you find yourself having time—I know things are done quickly—but do you find yourself having to make commercial decisions for the sake of time frames? You can think linearly in pop—what's the bass line gonna do and how can it be the most slick in the line that this makes, and it turns this into this inversion, and all of that—versus, just play it. Or do you worry about that?*

MP: Well, sometimes I do. What I do, I have to tell you and, boy, this is really the truth. I'm the luckiest guy that you'll ever talk to because I work best when I write the first thing that I feel or think and so . . .

CG: *That's how most sessions go anyway, after the first few times. Boy, it goes downhill after that.*

MP: I learned that as a player.

CG: *I learned that as a horn-session player. Man, if you don't get it soon, you'll be there all night.*

MP: Well, how many no brained g__ .... producers have ruined great performances by doing *take 23*?

CG: *Right!*

MP: I can just remember Sonny Bono—I was in the Sonny and Cher Band from *I Got You Babe* on—and I can remember him saying, "God, that was great—we need just one more." Well, if that one was great, why do you need just one more?

CG: *I have memories of people saying, "Give me more juice," talking "producerese."*

MP: Absolute mumbo jumbo horses... and in those days, of course—nowadays the guy with the most knowledge usually gets to say how it ought to be—but in those days it was like an A/R guy or some f..... tune guy and it just never made any musical sense. What I'm saying to you is I love the speed with which TV moves and eats music. I am not—I just haven't been raised musically to sit around and get anal about the linear counterpoint. F... it! Write a line, man. Stop talking and start writing.

CG: *So you're like Mozart. You're worried about putting something in the soprano voice and padding it!*

MP: Exactly, exactly. First of all we are not talking about molecular biology. We're talking about something that should just be created from the heart. I can sit around and intellectuallize, hopefully, with anybody in terms of counterpoint, etc., but the truth of the matter is, s---, I just wrote it.

CG: *The point of the book is to try to expose people to what's out there and how the process works, how the language works, and where they can begin. What is your advice to kids who have desire, and may have a large bag of innate skill, but have just got to learn and pay their dues—what do you want to tell them!*

MP: Well, first of all, I want to tell them that if they are immensly talented and focused, it is impossible for them not to make it.

CG: *I think that's true.*

MP: I mean it's impossible.

CG: *On some level.*

MP: That's what I'm saying. Then you have to define what's making it. Well, all I ever wanted to do was to make a living from music, I mean a good living. I wanted to support my family and be an honorable person and make a good living from music and, man, you can do that in any midlevel city in this country. Now you can really do it because of the "synth boogie." You can flat a--- do it. You got to be a pretty good programmer and you've got to sink some dough into some hardware and some software, but the truth of the matter is, God, you don't actually need players as long as you got a couple of them. Now, you're never gonna sound like a symphony, you're never gonna sound like a John Williams, you're never gonna sound like me unless you come to L.A. to do it on a film basis or you go to New York or Nashville on a record basis; but the truth of the matter is there's tremendous hope for young writers right now because there's so many avenues open to them, number one. Number two, if you sit down and logically look at the marketplace right now, you've got to see paradise because there are so many more outlets for film and so many more usages for music today than there were ten years ago and that just is true of every ten years back about fifty years. We're in the right place at the right time for what we do. Well, my viewpoint on it is that you cannot be a truly good film composer without being a damn good arranger, and those arranging skills are not beneficial—they're necessities. If you can't set it in the orchestra right, you're not worth a damn. All the hummers in the world aren't worth nothin'. There's a couple of them making it here right now in film. There's a couple of guys that are just lucky as hell. But the point is they are going to make a couple million bucks right now, but they ain't gonna last. The world is always going to belong to the Jerry Goldsmiths and the Dave Grusins and the Johnnie Williams and guys like that. Even the synth guys, everybody told me six or seven years ago when Jan Hammer showed up, "Ah, this is it. This is the new thing." I say, "Ah, bulls.... He's got a thing that he does really well, and it applies great to one show, and it's doing a great job on that one show—but you're going to get so tired of that one trick." If these synths are not folded in to the orchestra, it's worthless.

CG: *To what degree do you have to keep up with technology?*

MP: I'll tell you what I've done. It is so important to stay on the edge of that stuff, and I couldn't do it myself. The minute I took the mouse in my hand and started screwing around with the Performer myself, I blew it as a composer. I couldn't be explosive. I became a "gear head." The anal part of me that loves getting everything just perfect came out and it took me forever to mess with it myself. So I hired three young guys and all these guys do is manipulate the battlefield and get it ready for me to come in and compose just like I always have. So I sit down at my desk and I put a pencil in my hand and a piece of score paper underneath it and write the way I've always written. Then I take it in there and say, "OK, now what I had in mind was this from the d-50 and this from the 770 and this from the 8-rack and this and that. That's what I had in mind and this is how I want you to do it." Then I leave and when they get it ready, I come in there. The patient's open and ready on the table; I do heart surgery. Then I say, "Fellows, close him up," you know. And these three guys, in addition to actually manipulating and programming and engineering, they also have their binoculars on the ocean all the time so that anything new comes out, of course, I'm sitting on a pretty fat wallet—so I can afford to go and buy it, but that's what I do. These guys say, "Hey man, we need to have this now and we need to have that now" and I get it. I get it because you got to compete and in order to compete out there, you got to stay right on the edge of it.

CG: *Is there anything that I haven't asked you that you would like to say to people!*

MP: No, just that, the main thing that I say to any group of students that I speak to is that, boy, there is a great life to be had in writing music for film, and if you are truly great, there is a tremendous opportunity for you. All the people that tell you, "It's hard to get going and it's dog-eat-dog and there's no money in it," they're all crazy. It's a wide-open field. It's very easy for young people to get started today, much more so than ten years ago because you do not have to intern with somebody. You can come out here—and if you've got the right synth gear, you can demo for a thousand different projects and you can get your music heard by somebody. And if you're great, if you're truly special, you'll get hired. It's wide open right now. My song is a song of hope, boy—it is not black clouds. It is wide open and they are looking for young, hot people.

Bibliography

Baskerville, David. *Music Business Handbook and Career Guide.* Los Angeles: The Sherwood Company, 1985.

Coker, Jerry. *Improvising Jazz.* Englewood Cliffs, NJ: Prentice Hall, Inc., 1964.

Garcia, Russell. *The Professional Arranger Composer, Book 1.* Hollywood: Criterion Music Corporation, 1965.

_____. *The Professional Arranger Composer, Book 2.* Hollywood: Criterion Music Corporation, 1979.

Grove, Dick. *Arranging Concepts.* Sherman Oaks, CA: Alfred Publishing Co., Inc., 1975.

Hagen, Earle. *Scoring for Films.* Miami: E. D. J. Music, Inc., 1971.

Jaffe, Andrew. *Jazz Theory.* Dubuque, IA: Wm. C. Brown Company Publishers, 1983.

Karlin, Fred, and Rayburn Wright. *On the Track.* New York: Schirmer Books, 1990.

251

Mancini, Henry. *Sounds and Scores*. Port Chester, NY: Cherry Lane Books, 1973.

Marohnic, Chuck. *How to Create Jazz Chord Progressions*. Miami: Studio 224, 1979.

Norred, Larry Ross. *McChanges 1.0 Chord/Scale Parsing System*. USERsoft microSYSTEMS, 1989.

Piston, Walter. *Harmony*. New York: W. W. Norton & Company, Inc., 1987.

——————————. *Orchestration*. New York: W. W. Norton & Company, Inc., 1955.

Read, Gardner. *Thesaurus of Orchestral Devices*. Westport, CT: Greenwood Press, Publishers, 1969.

Riddle, Nelson. *Arranged By Nelson Riddle*. New York: Warner Bros. Publications, 1985.

Sample, Steve. *An Approach to Mainstream Jazz and Pop Harmony*. Tuscaloosa, AL: SOS Music Services, 1985.

Sebesky, Don. *The Contemporary Arranger*. Sherman Oaks, CA: Alfred Publishing Co., Inc., 1979.

Tanner, Paul O. W. and Maurice Gerow. *A Study of Jazz*. Dubuque, IA: Wm. C. Brown Company Publishers, 1981.

Turkel, Eric. *Arranging Techniques for Synthesists*. New York: Amsco Publications, 1988.

Wright, Rayburn. *Inside the Score*. Delevan, NY: Kendor, 1982.

Index

Accidentals, 14
Acoustic instruments, 161
Advertising, 147–51, 213–14
   226
Air horns, 164
Airtime, 147
Alka Seltzer, 217
Allen organs, 170
Alto voice, 172
Amnesty International, 219
Anticipation, 108, 112
Anvils, 164
Appoggiatura, 111
Aristotle, 9
Arrangement, 194
Arrangers, 188, 248
Artists, 198, 208–10
Art vs. craft, 205–6, 208–9
Audio, 225
Augmentation, 103
Augmented triads, 30
Authentic cadential move-
   ment, 74

Bach, J. S., 245
Ballads, 119

Band, The, 204
Bandleader, 207
Banjos, 172
Bass drums, 163
Basses 161, 172, 185, 191–92,
   242–43
Bassoons, 170
Bass voice, 172
Beatles, The, 203–4, 207
Beethoven, 196–97
Bells, 163
Berry, Chuck, 243
Big bands, 193, 197, 226
Big Dreamers Never Sleep,
   189
Black Cars, 186, 189
Black gospel, 119
"Blackjack Savage," 233
"Blossom," 240
Blues, 137–40
BMG, 189
Boat songs, 119
Bochco, Steven, 237
Bongos, 163
Bono, Sonny, 246
Borrowed harmony, 74

Bossa nova, 119–20
Bowing techniques, 165
Brass family, 165–67
Bridge, 144
Browne, Jackson, 207
Buffalo Springfield, 203–
   4

Cabasas, 163
Call and response, 139
Cambiata, 109
Canons, 164
Car horns, 164
Carlton, Larry, 239
Carpenter, Pete, 240
Castanets, 163
Castrati tenors, 172
Celestes, 163
Cellos, 165
Chariots of Fire, 219
Charles, Ray, 243
Chimes, 163
Chinese bell trees, 163
Chord changes, 242
Chord extensions, 44–50
Chord functions, 39–43

Chords, 26
   diatonic, 31–32
   dominant, 74
   dominant seventh, 46
   major seventh, 46
   neapolitan, 76
   $^9_6$, 50
   pivot, 71
   seventh, 33–34
   subdominant, 73
Chord spelling, 26–32
Chord substitutions, 73–78,
   80–88
Chord-symbol notation, 44
Chord voicings, 52–57
   closed position, 52
   clusters, 53, 55–56, 222
   drop 2, 53
   drop 2 and 4, 53–54
   open position, 53
   quartal, 54
Chorus, 143
Clapton, Eric, 195, 203
Clarinets, 168
Classical Gas, 244
Claves, 163
Clusters, 53, 55–56, 222
Cockburn, Bruce, 203
Col Legno, 165
Colvin, Shawn, 206
Commercials, 215, 222
Common tones, 58
Computers, 185, 226–27
Congas, 163
Constant relationships, 85–86
Constant structures, 86
Contemporary rock, 190
Corea, Chick, 225
Cornets, 165
Counterpoint, 186, 222, 227,
   246–47
Country, 198, 204, 210, 245
Cowbells, 163
Crazy Life, 185
Cross-rhythms, 119
Cycle of fifths, 64–66, 76–77
Cymbals, 163–64, 189

Dead cues, 219
Delayed attack, 113
Deteche, 165
Diatonic chords, 31
Diatonic extensions, 41
Diatonic inversion, 88
Diet Coke, 223
Diminished triads, 30
Diminution, 103
Dirges, 119
Dixieland jazz, 119
Dobros, 172, 240
Dr. John, 240
Documentary film, 154
Dominant, 41, 43
Donut, 149, 216
"Doogie Howser, M.D.," 233,
   239
Double basses, 165
Double reeds, 169–70
Double wind chimes, 163
Drinking songs, 119
Drummers, 186–87, 192
Drums, 161–63, 185, 243
Dvorak, Antonin, 244
Dylan, Bob, 193

Eastman (School of Music),
   225–26, 241
Echappee, 109
Electrical instruments, 185
Elevenths, 44, 46
End of Innocence, The, 206
English horns, 170
Enharmonic spelling, 48

Feature songs, 155, 157
Fifths, 29, 48
Films, 154
Film scoring, 151–53, 226
   closing credits, 154, 157,
   234
   credit music, 155
   end credits, 235
   hits, 152
   main title, 156, 234–36,
   240

   opening title, 154–55, 234
   score, 155, 234–37
   score for dialogue, 156
   themes, 155
Fish, 163
Flatted fifth, 48
Flatted thirteenth, 49
Flugelhorns, 165
Flutes, 167
Fogelberg, Dan, 199–200
   interview with, 201–10
Folk music, 207
Form, 192–94
   A-A-A, 143
   A-A-B, 145
   A-A1-B-A, 143
   A-B-A-B, 144
   A-B-A-C, 145
   A-B-C-D, 145
   and lyric, 195
   and structure, 194
Fourths, 7
Fragmentation, 105–6
French horns, 165
Frets, 171
Fretted instruments, 161,
   171–72
Funk, 119

Gabriel, Peter, 194
Gershwin, George, 195
Geyer, Stephen, 239
Gist of the Gemini, 187–88,
   190, 192
Glockenspiels, 163
Go-go bells, 163
Gold, Ernest, 239
Goldsmith, Jerry, 248
Gongs, 164
"Greatest American Hero,"
   239
Groove, 242–43
Grusin, Dave, 248
Guide tones, 59–61
Guiros, 163
Guitars, 172, 185, 202, 207,
   225, 239–40, 243

Half diminished, 35
Hammer, Jan, 248
Handmade key sets, 163
Harmonic motion, 39
Harmonic rhythm, 220
Harmonics, 165
Harmony, 138–39
Harmony techniques, 85–88
Harps, 171
Harpsichords, 171
Heavy-metal rock, 119
Henley, Don, 194, 206
"Hill Street Blues," 236–37,
    239
Hindemith, Paul, 241
Hook, 120, 148, 215–16
"Hunter," 234
Hymns, 119

"I Got You Babe," 246
Inconsolable Man, 189
Innocent Age, 204
Intervals, 1–8
    augmented fifth, 30
    augmented fourth, 7, 39
    compound, 7–8
    definition of, 1
    diatonic fifth, 48
    diminished fifth, 30, 39
    diminished fourth, 7
    diminished seventh, 35
    and harmonic motion, 39–
        40
    major second, 7
    major seventh, 35
    major third, 30
    minor seventh, 35
    minor third, 30
    Perfect, 7–8
    Perfect fifth, 7, 30
    Perfect fourth, 7
    seventh 34–35
Inversion of chords, 88
Inversion of notes, 104

Jazz, 190, 194, 225, 241
    big band, 190

gigs, 207
pianists, 197
players, 226
quartets, 191
trios, 187
waltzes, 119
Jete, 165
Jingles, 148–50, 216–18, 236
Johnson, Robert, 243

Keyboard instruments, 161,
    170
Keyboards, 226
Key signatures, 14–17
Kick drums, 163, 185

"L. A. Law," 233–34, 239
"Law and Order," 233, 239
Lawn mowers, 164
Leading tones, 19, 41
Lead sheets, 242
Leaps, 120–22
Les Miserables, 245
Light As A Feather, 225
Lightfoot, Gordon, 203
Linearly-based relationships,
    85
Liszt, Franz, 197
Loure, 165
Lullabies, 119
Lyrics, 184, 192–93, 203–4,
    239
Lyric scripts, 217
Lyric writing, 202

McDonald's, 217–18
Main motive, 120
Mainstream, 189
Major intervals, 7–8, 30
Major keys, 14
Mancini, Henry, 238, 240
Mandolins, 172
Maracas, 163
Marches, 119–20
Marimbas, 163
Markets, 214
Martellato, 165

Melodic contour, 118–24
Melodic release, 121–22
Melodic rhythm, 118–20
Melodic sequences, 106
Melodic shape, 121
Melody, 139–40, 192–93, 203–
    4, 206, 220, 226, 241, 243
    augmentation of, 103–4
    composition of, 123–24
    construction of, 99–100
    dimunition of, 103
    elements of, 100–104
    fragmentation of, 106
    inversion of, 104
    nonharmonic, 107–9
    phrase structure of, 122–23
    repetition of, 100–103
    retrograde in, 104
    from scales and modes,
        126–34
    structure of, 220, 236
    tension in, 121–22
    transposition of, 105
Meters, 114–15
MIDI, 226–27
Mini moog, 240
Minor intervals, 8, 30
Minor keys, 14
"Mission, The," 219
Mitchell, Joni, 203, 207
Modality, 9
Modes, 1, 9–10, 126, 133, 222,
    236
    aeolian, 10–11, 17, 127–28,
        132
    church, 10
    dorian, 10, 127, 129
    ionian, 10, 12, 126–27, 130,
        132
    locrian, 10–11, 127, 129,
        133
    lydian, 10–11, 127–28
    lydian ♭7, 129
    minor, 23, 222
    mixolydian, 10–11, 127–29
    phrygian mode, 10–11,
        127–28, 132

Modulations, 64–71
  Broadway, 66
  V and go, 67–68
  pivot-chord, 69–71
  prepared, 67, 69–70
  surprise, 67
Moussourgsky, Modest
  Petrovich, 207
Multiple stops, 165
Music
  Bulgarian, 245
  classical, 190, 194, 197
  commercial, 208
  Eastern, 190
  eastern European, 245
  ethnic, 244
  folk, 207
  Irish, 244–45
  Japanese, 190
  neoclassic, 241
  pop, 201
  rock, 119, 190, 204
Musica ficta, 19
Mutes, 165

Newman, Alfred, 238
Newman, Randy, 207
Newman method, 238
Ninths, 44–45
Nonharmonic tones, 61, 107
  accented passing tones,
    110–11
  anticipation, 107–8, 112
  appoggiatura, 110–11
  cambiata, 109
  changing tones, 107, 109
  echappee, 109
  escape tones, 107, 109
  "4-3" suspension, 110
  neighbor tones, 107–8
  "9-8" suspension, 110
  passing tones, 107
  suspended, 80
  suspended third, 110

Oboes, 170, 207
On The Track, 229

Orchestration, 161, 174–76,
  227, 238, 243
Ornamentation, 245
Oscillators, 175
Ostinato, 93–94

"Pad," 56, 59
Parallel major, 74
Parallel minor, 74
Parker, Charlie, 196
Partwriting, 59
Pauper In Paradise, A, 186,
  188
Pedal point, 90
Percussion family, 161–64,
  243
Phrases, 106, 122
Phrase structure, 122
Pianos, 171, 185, 192, 225
Piccolos, 167
Piccolo trumpets, 165
Pipe Organs, 170
Pizzacato, 165
Planing, 84
Plato, 9
Polkas, 119
Polychords, 83
Pop, 194, 201, 204, 242
Popular songs, 141–46, 201
Post, Mike, 219, 231–32
  interview with, 233–49
Powerful People, 191

"Quantum Leap," 234
Quartal, 53
Quarter and half tones, 190
Quartets, 186–87

Radio, 205–7, 214
Record companies, 189, 205–6
Relative major key, 66
Relative minor key, 66
Repetition, 100–101
Rhythm, 219–20, 223
Rhythmic displacement, 112
Ricochet, 165
Rimsky-Korsakoff, Nicolai, 207

Rockabilly, 119
Rock-and-roll, 185, 190, 241
Rock ballads, 242
"Rockford Files," 240
Rock music, 119, 190, 204
Root position, 74
Roots, 26, 29
Roto toms, 163
Royal Philharmonic, 187

Saltando, 165
Saltato, 165
Samba, 119–20, 242
"Same Old Lang Syne," 205
Sample film footage, 151–52
Samplers, 226
Sampling, 175–76
Saxophones, 168–69, 207
Scales, 1, 9–25
  ascending melodic minor,
    130
  blues, 131, 139
  descending melodic minor,
    131
  diminished, 24, 55–56
  diminished half-whole, 25,
    131
  diminished whole-half, 25,
    132
  harmonic minor, 19, 23,
    32, 35, 130
  Hindu, 134
  locrian sharp 2, 133
  lydian diminished, 133
  major, 1, 5, 12
  major pentatonic, 24, 131
  melodic minor, 19, 21, 23
  minor, 17
  minor pentatonic, 24, 131
  natural minor, 10, 17–19,
    23, 35, 131
  pentatonic, 24
  whole-tone, 24, 55, 132
Scene changes, 236
Sebesky, Don, 187–88
Secondary area principle, 81
Secondary dominant, 75

Sequences, 106
Sequencing, 176
Sharped eleventh, 46, 48
Sharped fifth, 48
Shostakovitch, Dimitri, 244–45
"Shots," 59
Simon, Paul, 194–95, 203
Single reeds, 167–68
Sitars, 172
Sixth scale degree, 49
Skips, 121–22
Sleigh bells, 163
Slogans, 150
Snare drums, 162
Song cycles, 204–5
Songs, 185–86, 191–92, 202–3
Songwriters, 203, 208
Songwriting, 201–2, 206, 226
Sonny and Cher, 246
Soprano voice, 161, 172
Sound effects, 221–22
Sound scape, 222
Spiccato, 165
"Spots," 147, 149, 234
Staccato, 165
Standard, 141–42, 157
Sting, 194, 205
Stings, 235
Storm At Sunup, 187, 192
Storyboards, 151–52, 213, 218–20
Stravinsky, Igor, 196, 241
String family, 165, 237
Subdominant, 42–43
Sul ponticello, 165
Sul tasto, 165
Swing, 119
Swing shuffle, 119
Syncopation, 113
Synthesizers, 175, 187–88, 214

Tchaikovsky, Peter Ilyich, 207

Technology, 185–86, 203, 226, 230, 248
Television, 224, 232, 246
Television shows, 154–55, 233–35
Temple blocks, 163
Tempo, 236–37
Tenor voice, 172
Tension, 121–22
Texture, 188, 227
Thirds, 29
Thirdstream, 190
Thirteenths, 44, 48
Thompson, J. Walter, 214
Timbales, 163
Timbre, 223
Time signatures, 114–15
Timing breakdowns, 152
Timpani, 163
Tom-toms, 162
Tonality, 73
Tones
    accented passing, 111
    changing, 109
    common, 58–59
    escape, 109
    neighbor, 108
    nonharmonic, 107–12
    passing, 107
Tonic, 40, 43
Top 40 radio, 201, 206
Top ten, 189
Train whistles, 164
Transposition, 105
Tremolos, 165
Triads
    augmented, 26, 30
    construction of, 27–29
    definition of, 26
    diminished, 26, 30–31, 35
    major, 26, 30–31
    minor, 26, 30–31, 47
    types of, 30–31

Triangles, 163
Trills, 165
Tritones, 39–40
Trombones, 165
Trumpets, 166
Tubas, 165
Tubular bells, 163

Ukeleles, 172
Underscore, 154

Vannelli, Gino, 1, 181–82
    interview with, 183–98
Variant set, 85
Variant structure, 87
Verse, 143
Vertical relationships, 85–86
Vibraphones, 163
Vibra slaps, 163
Vie Records, 189
Violas, 165
Violins, 165, 243
Voice family, 161, 172, 191
Voice leading, 58–62
Voice-overs, 224
Voice performance, 203

Waltzes, 119
When You Wish Upon a Star, 218
Whips, 164
Wilde, Doug, 1, 211–12
    interview with, 213–30
Williams, John, 247–48
Wind chimes, 163
Woodblocks, 163
Woodwind family, 161, 167
Work prints, 152
Work songs, 119
Wright, Ray, 229

Xylophones, 163